# LEADERS *on* LEADERSHIP

TWELVE PERSONAL REFLECTIONS ON THE THEME OF LEADERSHIP

# LEADERS *on* LEADERSHIP

Edited by Stuart Crainer, with a foreword by
HRH The Prince Philip, Duke of Edinburgh KG, KT

the Institute
of Management
FOUNDATION

Copyright © IM

First Published 1996

The Institute of Management
Management House
Cottingham Road
Corby
Northants
NN17 1TT

British Library Cataloguing in Publication Data

A CIP catalogue record for this report is available from the British Library

ISBN 085946-267-6

Printed and bound in Great Britain by
Biddles Ltd, Guildford and King's Lynn

the Institute
of Management

*FOUNDATION*

*The Mission of the Institute of Management is to promote the development, exercise and recognition of professional management.*

Representing over 70,000 UK and world-wide members, the Institute of Management is the professional body for managers. Members come from all sectors, both public and private, and all levels of responsibility, from supervisor to Chief Executive. Membership is offered on both and individual and a corporate basis.

These are just some of the benefits of membership:

- ◆ Preferential rates for all IM books, reports and computer software

- ◆ Professional advice on all aspects of employment, redundancy and pensions

- ◆ Individual career counselling to help you plan your career

- ◆ A recruitment service to put you in touch with suitable vacancies

- ◆ More than 100 UK branches for the exchange of views and experiences

- ◆ Free copies of Britain's leading management journals

- ◆ Access to the largest management information centre in Europe

However, as a leading supplier of management education and training in the UK we also offer

- ◆ Courses and seminars to keep you up to date with the latest management skills and techniques

- ◆ In-company training and consultancy tailored specifically to your own organisations needs

- ◆ Management development programmes to develop your skills, leading to the award of NVQ/SVQ's and/ or an IM Certificate and Diploma in Management

For further information contact the **Marketing Department**:

**The Institute of Management**
Management House
Cottingham Road
Corby
Northants NN17 1TT

Tel: 01536 204222
Fax: 01536 201651
Email: institute@easynet.co.uk.

# CONTENTS

## BUCKINGHAM PALACE.

# FOREWORD

It is relatively easy to identify successful leaders, it is rather more complicated to describe what constitutes good leadership. For one thing leadership is exercised in so many different ways and under many different circumstances. Even leadership in the armed services varies considerably. "Come on lads, follow me" may be a suitable way to exercise leadership of a platoon in battle, but something different is needed to lead a squadron of aircraft or to take a ship into action and to ensure that its crew makes the most effective use of its equipment to engage the enemy. Both those forms of leadership have to be developed long before they are put to the test.

The founders of successful companies may be natural leaders, but they will encounter a wide variety of challenges to their leadership as their companies develop and grow. A chairman of a voluntary organisation will be leading in quite a different way. The problem, therefore, about discussing leadership in general is to identify those qualities that are common to all its different forms.

Deciding on a course of action and leading from in front is the most apparent form of leadership, but there is probably more skill in gaining consensus among a board composed of executive and non-executive directors, a diverse workforce or among a group of trustees of a voluntary organisation. Political leaders have an even more difficult task of satisfying their party members and gaining the support of the voters.

Initiative is obviously a common factor, as is the capacity for original thinking and problem solving. Willingness to accept responsibility and a talent for achieving consensus might be added to the list, but I suspect one vital factor is the indefinable quality of character that creates confidence and motivates and inspires others to follow or to agree.

Perhaps the most important talent needed by anyone aspiring to be a leader is good judgement. Important decisions usually have to be made very quickly and they have to be seen as having been the right ones - at least more often than not. Napoleon is said to have asked for 'lucky' generals. Whether getting it right is a matter of luck or good judgement, one thing is certain, anyone who gets things wrong and fails to learn from their mistakes is never likely to make a good leader.

# Introduction

People are perennially fascinated by leaders and leadership but find the nature of leadership impossibly elusive. Few subjects have been as extensively examined, but for all the books, seminars and discussions, consensus is rarely found.

Ask any group of people to name a number of leaders and they are as likely to name Stalin as Mother Teresa; Neil Armstrong as John Harvey-Jones; and Mahatma Gandhi as Fidel Castro. And a question on what skills and attributes are required of a leader is likely to yield a similarly diverse response: vision, inspiration, determination, stubbornness and ability to communicate tend to be among the most common. Yet leadership stereotypes are riddled with exceptions. There is no formula for leadership. Lists of personality traits do not prepare people for the full scope and range of what leadership entails and what people expect from their leaders.

Leadership has been exercised - and thought about - since the very start of civilisation. The Chinese philosopher Lao Tze was writing about leadership 2,500 years ago and astonishingly, his work is still referred to. (This, according to your views, can be attributed to the timelessness of his ideas; or the paucity of original modern thinking in this area.) It is only in recent years that leadership has re-emerged as a topic worthy of serious debate and discussion. Previously, there was a tendency to assume that leadership is one of those mystically intangible qualities with which some people are blessed and which others miss out on. Alternatively, it has been thought that leadership is the sole preserve of soldiers, politicians, religious figures and a select few sports people. Today, however, the vital role performed by leaders in the business world is increasingly recognised, analysed and, sometimes, understood.

This does not mean that there is now a cut-and-dried workable and all-embracing definition of what leadership is, what it involves or who should practise it. Life and leadership are rarely so straightforward. One estimate puts the number of leadership definitions at over 400. It is a veritable minefield of misunderstanding and difference through which theorists and practitioners must tread warily.

The literal meaning of leadership perhaps provides as safe a starting point as any. Though the word leadership first appeared in English in 1300, it was not commonly used until the nineteenth century. In English, at least, the semantics ensure that leadership and management remain separated. Others are not so sure - in German 'fuhrüngskunst' can be translated as both.

British leadership expert, John Adair, has observed: 'Leadership is about a sense of direction. The word *lead* comes from an Anglo-Saxon word, common to north

European languages, which means a road, a way, the path of a ship at sea. It's knowing what the next step is.'[1] Adair differentiates leadership from management - the latter, he contends, is rooted in mechanics, control and systems. He has defined leadership as three circles which overlap. These circles embody what he labels 'task, team and individual'.

## What do leaders do?

In their book, *The Leadership Challenge*, the Americans James Kouzes and Barry Posner identify five characteristics of what they called 'exemplary' leaders. These are:

1. **Leaders challenge the process.** Leaders search for opportunities. They experiment and take risks, constantly challenging other people to exceed their own limitations.

2. **Leaders inspire a shared vision.** Leaders envision an ennobling future and enlist people to join in that new direction.

3. **Leaders enable others to act.** Leaders strengthen others and foster collaboration.

4. **Leaders model the way.** Leaders set the example for people by their own leadership behaviour, and they plan small wins to get the process moving.

5. **Leaders encourage the heart.** Leaders regard and recognise individual contributions and they celebrate team successes.[2]

There are numerous other such checklists - of varying usefulness and, it must be said, plausibility. One of the most frequently quoted is from Warren Bennis and Burt Nanus' 1985 bestseller *Leaders: The Strategies for Taking Charge*. This examines the behaviour and characteristics of 90 leaders and seeks to reach general conclusions. The leaders studied were a truly eclectic - and somewhat eccentric - group, including Neil Armstrong and Karl Wallenda, a tight-rope walker. Bennis and Nanus concluded that the leaders possessed four vital competencies:

- ◆ **management of attention** - the vision of the leaders commanded the attention and commitment of those who worked for and with them in attempting to achieve it.

- ◆ **management of meaning** - the leaders were skilled communicators, able to cut through complexity to frame issues in simple images and language. They were expert distillers of information.

- ◆ **management of trust** - 'Trust is essential to all organisations,' observes Bennis. For the leaders, trust was expressed through consistency of purpose and in their dealings with colleagues and others. Even though people sometimes disagreed with what they said or did, the leaders were admired for their consistency of purpose.

- ◆ **management of self** - the leaders were adept at identifying and fully utilising their strengths; and accepting and seeking to develop areas of weakness.

While Bennis' work has sought out a broad perspective on leadership, John Adair provides a list based on the day-to-day reality of business. In *Understanding Motivation*, Adair identifies the functions of leadership as:

♦ **Planning** - seeking all available information; defining group tasks or goals; making a workable plan

♦ **Initiating** - briefing the group; allocating tasks; setting group standards

♦ **Controlling** - maintaining group standards; ensuring progress towards objectives; 'prodding' actions and decisions

♦ **Supporting** - expressing acceptance of individual contributions; encouraging and disciplining; creating team spirit; relieving tension with humour; reconciling disagreements

♦ **Informing** - clarifying task and plan; keeping the group informed; receiving information from the group; summarising ideas and suggestions

♦ **Evaluating** - checking feasibility of ideas; testing consequences; evaluating group performance, helping the group to evaluate itself.[3]

Such lists suggest that today's business leaders need to be Renaissance men and women, corporate super heroes. They must be continually on the move, changing chameleon-like from one incarnation to another, from coach to objective critic, from summariser to inspirer.

However, there is hope. Adair, formerly a lecturer at Sandhurst Military Academy, argues that leadership skills can be learned and developed. Whether this is possible or not lies at the heart of a great many of the debates on the subject of leadership.

Not surprisingly, military leaders tend to argue that leadership is often an innate quality which simply needs to be given the right conditions in which to thrive. Military training is designed to create these conditions. Explorer, expedition organiser and former soldier, Sir John Blashford-Snell, now organises training expeditions for managers. 'We want them to develop their leadership skills and themselves. Communication and inspiration are the keys to leadership. Giving managers a task, such as trapping a python in a dark building to find out how much it weighs, you quickly discover people's skills and how they respond to unusual situations,' he says. 'The expeditions often re-vitalise people and give them a new perspective on themselves and what they do. Many people have a spark of what it takes to lead. On an expedition this spark can be turned into a flame.' To Blashford-Snell it is simply a question of creating the opportunity for people to experience new situations and to be aware of how they respond. Leadership is there - it is a matter of allowing people to find it and use it.

## *Machiavellian leadership*

While some seek out their leadership qualities in the wild others turn to leadership literature for clarification. Here, too, the number of potential sources is intimidatingly vast. The contemporary leader is as likely to find relevant pearls of wisdom in Machiavelli as in Tom Peters.

Amid the grey-suited pantheon of leadership thinkers, Nicoló Machiavelli (1469-1527) holds an unlikely, but undeniable, place. A Florentine diplomat and writer, his career was colourful - punctuated by interludes of indulgence in 'petty dissipations', torture on the rack and farming. His abiding relevance to the world of leadership rests on a slim volume, *The Prince*.

*The Prince* is the sixteenth century equivalent of Dale Carnegie's *How to Make Friends and Influence People*. Embedded beneath details of Alexander VI's tribulations, lie a ready supply of aphorisms and insights which are, perhaps sadly, as appropriate to many of today's leaders and organisations as they were nearly 500 years ago. Machiavelli exposes the all too human under-belly of leadership.

'It is unnecessary for a prince to have all the good qualities I have enumerated, but it is very necessary to appear to have them,' Machiavelli advises, adding the suggestion that it is useful 'to be a great pretender and dissembler'. But *The Prince* goes beyond such helpful presentational hints. Like all great books, it offers something for everyone. Take Machiavelli on managing change: 'There is nothing more difficult to take in hand, more perilous to conduct, or more uncertain in its success, than to take the lead in the introduction of a new order of things.' Or on sustaining motivation: 'He ought above all things to keep his men well-organised and drilled, to follow incessantly the chase.'

Above all, Machiavelli is the champion of leadership through cunning and intrigue, the triumph of force over reason. An admirer of Borgia, Machiavelli had a dismal view of human nature. Empowerment was not in his vocabulary. Unfortunately, as he sagely points out, history has repeatedly proved that a combination of being armed to the teeth and devious is more likely to allow you to achieve your objectives. It is all very well being good, says Machiavelli, but the leader 'should know how to enter into evil when necessity commands'.

'Like the leaders Machiavelli sought to defend, some executives tend to see themselves as the natural rulers in whose hands organisations can be safely entrusted,' says psychologist Robert Sharrock of consultants YSC. 'Theories abound on their motivation. Is it a defensive reaction against failure or a need for predictability through complete control? The effect of the power-driven Machiavellian manager is usually plain to see.'

In companies addicted to internal politics, Machiavelli remains the stuff of day-to-day reality. But, warns Robert Sharrock, Machiavellian management may have had its day. 'The gentle art of persuasion is finding fashion with managers. The ends no longer justify the means. The means, the subtle management of relationships, are the ends by which future opportunities may be created. Also, most managers now recognise that organisations have purposes other than the maximisation of profit. There is a return to the age of reason against which Machiavelli rebelled.'

For many the age of reason has yet to dawn. Managers may not have read *The Prince* but will be able to identify with Machiavelli's observation that 'a prince ought to have no other aim or thought, nor select anything else for his study, than war and its rules and discipline'.

## Modern words of wisdom

Modern thinkers tend to overlook the world of human darkness inhabited by Machiavelli. Leadership is seen in a more positive light. Book after book attempts to establish links between successful leaders. Many are unconvincingly selective or plainly optimistic.

If there is any common thread it is that successful leaders have a bias towards action. They are dynamic and energetic achievers; the kind of people who would relish the challenge of capturing a python in a darkened room. Even the most cerebral of leaders appears to possess a need to prove his or her point energetically or even physically. It is notable that business leaders often have international experience early in their career or acquire a wide range of experience through travel or working in a number of jobs and situations. They are restlessly inquisitive.

Warren Bennis has observed that 'more leaders have been made by accident, circumstance, sheer grit or will than have been made by all the leadership courses put together'. Indeed, Bennis has been candid enough to admit that his own experience of actually leading an organisation proved infinitely more demanding than he anticipated. He interrupted his academic career to become a provost at the State University of New York at Buffalo and then president of the University of Cincinnati. This proved disappointing. 'The very time I had the most power, I felt the greatest sense of powerlessness,' Bennis observes in the autobiographical *An Invented Life*. In practice, Bennis found that his ambitious intentions were hamstrung by the very organisation he purported to lead. Despite the power attributed to him through his job title, in practice he was powerless. All the theories in the world do not make for effective leadership.

Indeed, in the world of leadership the gulf between theory and practice is cavernous. 'In education it is important that students connect what they learn to what they actually do. Executive education goes on every day, not simply by sending executives to a classroom. Too much formal executive education reinforces the status quo of the organisation and too many academics are romantic in the pejorative sense. They run away from developing new approaches so you read 600 pages on leadership and it adds up to what? There are academic standards, but theories need to be tested,' says Harvard Business School's Chris Argyris. 'Academics and executives have a love-hate relationship. Academics say that executives are too shallow; while executives are interested in the pay-off. What executives now complain about is not the newness of the concepts but that the new concepts don't keep implementation in mind. You get unconnected fads and ideas so that managers can't use them.'

The theory and practice conundrum perhaps proves that there can be nothing clinical about leadership. It is this highly personal, individual and energetic side of leadership which can serve to confuse and encourage. These elements appear to be deeply bedded in power rather than goodness. Unfortunately, history repeatedly proves that great leaders are not necessarily good, righteous, moral, humane or fair. Some are evil, but that does not stop them being formidable leaders - and nor should it detract from the achievements of those leaders with some measure of goodness on their side.

David Gilbert-Smith, founder of the Leadership Trust and another former military man, points to the need for leaders to be sure of themselves before they begin to mobilise and inspire others. 'I realised very early that true leadership comes not from rank or status but from personal power. The raw material of leadership is human nature. In the study of leadership our own nature is both subject and object,' he says. 'Leadership means winning people's hearts and minds. To do so requires first winning one's own. So leadership development begins with the confidence of self-knowledge and the calm of self-control. These are qualities which can be developed, not easily, not by mechanical application of any "leadership theory", but by looking long, hard, truthfully at our behaviour and our effect on others and then -crucially - committing oneself to the personal responsibility for doing something about it.' This view suggests that the true leader is acutely self-aware, able to take an objective view of his or her own talents and humble enough to identify and seek to remedy areas of weakness.

14

## Defining moments

While hard and fast definitions are difficult to come by, there are a whole host of pithy aphorisms which capture some aspects of what leadership entails. They are often attractively memorable, while not always being highly practical. In *The Tao of Leadership*, John Heider observes: 'The wise leader does not push to make things happen but allows the process to unfold on its own. The leader knows that constant interventions will block the group's process.' Perhaps more pointedly, Warren Bennis, came up with the conclusion that 'managers do things right. Leaders do the right thing'. Charles Handy says: 'A leader shapes and shares a vision, which gives point to the work of others.' There are many other similar codas to the practice of leadership. These prove the diversity of interpretation while giving some flavour of how personal and unique leadership can be.

To those in the real and immediate world of business such wisdom can appear ethereal and distant. Business and management seek out solid foundations; tools and techniques rather than ideas. As a result, in the business world traditional views of leadership are strongly rooted in the command and control system of management. They revere authority above all and identify leadership as a weapon only for the use of very senior executives. 'Managers have been brought up on a diet of power, divide and rule. They have been preoccupied with authority rather than making things happen,' says Charles Handy. The conventional inspiration lies with military role models - generals forming brilliant strategies implemented by compliant armies. Success is equated with being granted heroic status. Heroes stand out above the crowd, offering panoramic visions of the future and then proceed to walk all over anything in the way.

The traditional view was - and is - based around the fundamental beliefs that the leader is right and that coercion and physical rewards are necessary to persuade people to put the leader's 'right' decision into practice. This encounters difficulties when the leader is wrong and force, or the exercise of power, cannot motivate people to do something they don't believe in or know will fail.

## The model leader of the 1990s

American social psychologist and researcher Rensis Likert identified four basic management styles: exploitative authoritarian; benevolent authoritarian; consultative; and participative. Much management practice has been resolutely based within the authoritarian camp. Though command and control lives on in many organisations, the deficiencies of this authority-based approach are increasingly clear.

When John F Kennedy met a group of business people in his early days at the White House, one told him that what the country needed was a 'man on horseback' who could sweep away competitors and opposition. In response Kennedy argued that, in peace-time, leadership is not about destroying the opposition. Instead, leadership is concerned with building bridges and setting a new agenda.

In the new world order of hyper-competition, forget the man on horseback. Leadership has to be more pragmatic and flexible than being entirely reliant on power and authority. It has to move and adapt. Leaders such as Eisenhower and de Gaulle were, for example, able to make the switch from being war-time leaders to leaders of the peace. Their style of leadership was capable of transformation.

American consultant and author, Don Laurie has examined the current nature of leadership - including interviews with 20 of the world's top executives. 'There is a need for a contemporary theory of leadership to provide a framework for mobilising people,' says Laurie. 'In my experience, too many managers describe the work of the leader with a series of clichés: 'to provide vision', 'to set direction', 'to motivate people,' etc. In practice, senior executives and managers seem to respond pragmatically to problems - calling on their own experience, common sense and selected management principles they have come to believe in over the years. Beyond this, the terms 'leadership', 'authority' and 'power' tend to be used interchangeably and in a sloppy way.'[4]

The message is that what once constituted a great leader may not be the recipe for managerial success in the empowered 1990s. 'The leader's role has changed. It has become more complex and arguably even more critical to success,' says Peter Phillips, head of leadership programmes at BP. 'Leaders must ensure that high performance levels are achieved and sustained; handle complexity and ambiguity; enjoy leading the change process; ensure that the organisation and its processes constantly develop; and that people within the company are motivated, developed and rewarded to produce outstanding results.'

To help develop its leaders, BP has a leadership competency model and development framework. But is this too structured a means of identifying and nurturing tomorrow's leaders? Peter Phillips contends that any system must be able to cope with individualism: 'Individuality, flexibility and scope for mavericks must be retained. The purpose of the development framework is to identify and develop the leaders who will deliver performance today and in the future. The aim is to let talent develop and flourish not to clone leaders.'

### The leader as team player

Instead of being an isolated and glorious figurehead, the new model leader is part of a team. 'In some cases, the needs of a situation bring to the fore individuals with unique qualities or values, however, most leaders have to fit their skills, experience and vision to a particular time and place', says psychologist Robert Sharrock. 'Today's leaders have to be pragmatic and flexible to survive. Increasingly, this means being people rather than task-oriented. The great man theory about leadership rarely applies - if teams are what make businesses run, then we have to look beyond individual leaders to groups of people with a variety of leadership skills.'

No leader can act in isolation - though they may like to think that they can. In fact, the achievements of leaders are always the achievements of many. As one commentator caustically observed: 'Without an army, Napoleon was just a man with a hat.' Followers and leaders need each other to survive and prosper. Leaders who forget this do so at their peril.

New outlooks on leadership place greater emphasis on the role of followers and the relationship between leaders and followers. 'Followers are becoming more powerful. It is now common for the performance of bosses to be scrutinised and appraised by their corporate followers. This, of course, means that leaders have to actively seek the support of their followers in a way they would never have previously contemplated,' says Robert Sharrock.

New definitions also bring in followers -'Leadership is a process of influence between a leader and those who are followers'[5]; 'The new leader...is one who commits people to action, who converts followers into leaders, and who may convert leaders into agents of change.'[6]

The leader is increasingly regarded as an **integrator** - rather than as a divider or commander. In *The Working Leader,* Leonard Sayles of MIT focuses on the middle manager as leader rather than the pantheon of heroic corporate leaders, such as John Harvey-Jones or Jack Welch in the US. In Sayles' view the role of leadership is neither to inspire nor to make astute decisions, but to integrate the disparate elements of the system. While functions, jobs and departments tend to splinter it is leadership which can integrate and bring things back together. Sayles defines his concept of 'work leadership' as 'the ability to keep adapting, modifying, adjusting and rearranging the complex task and function interfaces that keep slipping out of alignment'.[7]

Sayles takes a step back from the conventional view of leadership as concerned with vision and the ability to influence and inspire. Instead, the leader provides a kind of corporate adhesive, bringing people and functions together.

Leonard Sayles' world view does not sound the death knell for leadership. It simply means that in the 1990s and beyond different types of leadership skills will be required in the business world and elsewhere. New leaders will emerge with completely different role models and leadership aspirations.

Examining the behaviour of a number of top managers, Ashridge Management College's Phil Hodgson concluded that the managers acted as resources rather than as traditional authoritarian leaders: 'The high performers do not appear to be concerned with who gets the credit. Nor are they caught in a hierarchical straitjacket. They are willing to take part as an equal in group discussions and are anxious that their colleagues regard then as a resource, a conduit to more information, or a problem-solver.' It would be difficult to imagine someone like Henry Ford or other corporate giants from the past acting as a 'resource'. Echoing Leonard Sayles' conclusions, Ashridge's Hodgson says: 'Generally, the high performers had outgrown the notion of the individualistic leader, striving to lead by impressive example. Instead, they regarded leadership as a question of drawing people together and pulling disparate parts of the organisation together in a way that made individuals and the organisation more effective.' He concludes that the work of the new leader is characterised by:

- ◆ adding value as a coach, mentor and problem solver rather than as a source of interference

- ◆ allowing people to accept credit for success... and responsibility for failure

- ◆ considering, evaluating and enhancing their own leadership role on a continuous basis

- following no rigid or orthodox role models, preferring to nurture their own unique leadership style

- not indulging in leadership by continual practical example (doing people's jobs for them) or personality cult

- continually investing time in people -colleagues, employees, suppliers and customers

- managing on a personal, often face-to-face basis continually and naturally.[8]

The magic which marks the new leaders apart has been analysed by INSEAD leadership expert, Manfred Kets de Vries. 'They go beyond narrow definitions. They have an ability to excite people in their organisations,' he says. 'They also work extremely hard - leading by example is not dead - and are highly resistant to stress. Also, leaders like Richard Branson and Percy Barnevik are very aware of what their failings are. They make sure that they find good people who can fill these areas.' In the age of empowerment, the ability to delegate effectively is critically important. 'Empowerment and leadership are not mutually exclusive,' says Professor de Vries. 'The trouble is that many executives feel it is good to have control. They become addicted to power - and that is what kills companies.'

This is strikingly different from accepted and traditional roles mapped out for business leaders. It does, however, fit in with many of the trends within management. Research by the Institute of Management, *Management Development to the Millennium*, surveyed over 1,200 managers, asking them which skills they thought would be required in the future.

| Priority | Most important skills | % respondents |
|----------|----------------------|---------------|
| 1 | Strategic thinking (eg longer term, broader perspective, anticipating) | 78 |
| 2 | Responding to and managing change | 75 |
| 3 | An orientation towards total quality and customer satisfaction | 67 |
| 4 | Financial management (eg role and impact of key financial indicators) | 46 |
| 5 | Facilitating others to contribute | 44 |
| 6 | Understanding the role of information and IT | 42 |
| 7 | Verbal communication (eg coherent, persuasive) | 38 |
| 8 | Organisational sensitivity (eg cross functional understanding) | 37 |
| 9 | Risk assessment in decision making | 35 |

*Figure 1: Management skills for the future*

Some of these skills rest comfortably within conventional notions of business leadership. These include strategic thinking, financial management and risk assessment. Others, however, demonstrate the need for changes in the behaviour and skills of leaders. The leaders of the past did not have to contend with aspects such as 'facilitating others to contribute' or have to further cross-functional understanding. 'A new kind of leader has emerged who is a facilitator, not an autocrat, an appreciator of ideas, not necessarily a fount of them. The Great Man - or Woman - still exists as the public face of companies and countries, but the leader and the organisation are no longer one and the same,' writes Warren Bennis. 'Around the world, the generals are being ousted and the poets are taking charge.'

This is a colourful image. But it does make an important point for leadership to the end of the century. From being strategy-driven, leadership has become a more creative and positive approach driven by persuasion rather than power. 'The old hierarchical model is no longer appropriate. The new model is global in scale, an interdependent network. So the new leader faces new tests, such as how does he lead people who don't report to him -people in other companies, in Japan or Europe, even competitors. How do you lead in this idea-intensive, interdependent-network environment?' John Sculley, former CEO of Apple, has asked. 'It requires a wholly different set of skills based on ideas, people skills, and values. Traditional leaders are having a hard time explaining what's going on in the world, because they're basing their explanations on their experience with the old paradigm.'[9]

## The vision thing

In a business climate beset by change, leadership too must change. There is, however, one element which unites past and present conceptions of leadership: a sense of vision. Visions set the tone for organisations and carry them forward. 'One of the first duties is to create what I call atmosphere,' observed the military leader Montgomery. John Harvey-Jones followed a similar process with ICI. When the company announced its first-ever quarterly loss, Harvey-Jones could have retreated into a defensive shell. Instead, he determined to take the company boldly forward and set its target as achieving the first billion-pound profit by a UK industrial company. The vision was ambitious - apparently overly ambitious - but one which Harvey-Jones correctly calculated would galvanise people into action.

The problem with creating - and living - powerful, persuasive visions is that they must carry people with them. In recent years there have been a number of well-documented cases where top managers have lost their jobs following a failure to convince others of the merit of their visions. Their visions of the future were ambitious, credible and possibly achievable, but it did not seem so to their colleagues and subordinates. Instead, all their colleagues could see was a long line of obstacles and impediments to achieving the distant goal. The disenchantment of their people eventually cost the chief executives their jobs. Without followers they became merely men with hats.

To work, visions must motivate and sustain people through their implementation. In General Electric's 1990 annual report, chief executive Jack Welch mapped out the company's vision: 'Our dream for the 1990s is a boundaryless company....where we knock down the walls that separate us from each other on the inside and from our key constituents on the outside.' Welch is transforming GE, breaking down barriers, bringing corporate leaders into direct contact -and conflict - with those affected by their decisions.

As Welch is proving, vision is not an ethereal concept. Leaders must bridge the gap between the noble aspirations of the vision and the day-to-day reality. As visionaries, leaders must:

- seem to have as much to lose by not leading the organisation forward as those they lead

- be able to give hope to people when it seems impossible that they will find their way out

- act out the vision and be a role model so people can see it active and embodied and be able to copy or reproduce it

- challenge and practise

- care personally

- take from people offerings, ideas and efforts which lead towards the vision.

It is a two-way and continuous process. Leaders who ignore this do so at their peril and, in the end, are unlikely to succeed.

26      Conclusions about the nature of leadership will continue to be wildly different. But, what can be said categorically is that leadership is a powerful force. It can - and does - invigorate and drive businesses; it runs countries, government departments and inspires sports teams. It revolutionises the performance of both individuals and large multi-national organisations. While its power cannot be doubted, it is how this power is channelled which is of paramount importance.

*Stuart Crainer*

*References*

1. Adair, J, *The Director*, November 1988

2. Kouzes, JM, & Posner, BZ, *The Leadership Challenge: How to get Extraordinary Things Done in Organizations*, Jossey-Bass, San Fransisco, 1987

3. Adair, J, *Understanding Motivation*, Talbot Adair, Guildford, 1990

4. Laurie, D, 'Leadership & Management', in *The Financial Times Handbook of Management*, FT/Pitman, London, 1995

5. Hollander, EP, *Leadership Dynamics*, Free Press, New York, 1978

6. Bennis, Warren, and Nanus, Burt, *Leaders: Strategies for Taking Charge*, Harper & Row, New York, 1985

7. Sayles, L, *The Working Leader*, The Free Press, New York, 1993

8. Hodgson, P, & Crainer, S, *What do high performance managers really do?*, FT/Pitman, London, 1993

9. Quoted in Bennis, W, *An Invented Life*, Addison Wesley, Reading, Mass, 1993

27

# SIR PETER PARKER

*On Leadership*

---

*Sir Peter Parker* KBE LVO CIMgt *is currently chairman of a number of companies which include Mitsubishi Electric UK.*

A Major in the Intelligence Corps during the Second World War, he has extensive leadership experience. Sir Peter Parker served as Chairman of the British Institute of Management from 1984 to 1986, and has received several notable awards including Communicator of the year. He remains best known for his seven years as chairman of British Rail (1976-1983). Sir Peter's autobiography, *For Starters*, was a bestseller.

Leadership is one of those humpty-dumpty words Alice in Wonderland defined as meaning whatever we want them to mean. Yet these days nothing makes more of a buzz in business circles. There must be something therapeutic in that we talk so much about it - therapeutic and dangerous.

It makes us feel good because it is a relief, and it is a relief because the sheer idea of leadership reminds us of the sheer humanity of management, the mystery, the charisma. Professional management has to spend much of its time measuring and controlling, quite properly. But we all know those over-muscled, bureaucratic organisations where there seems to be plenty of snaffle and bit, but where's the bloody horse? So we find ourselves enjoying the scope to speculate about leadership, and how it happens. Is it education or lack of it, sensitivity or insensitivity? Will, guts or just wanting money very, very much? I find that there are no absolutes, no models.

A study of 300 successful senior managers by Dr Rob Irving of the Whitehead Mann Group found that these managers were not exceptional when measured in terms of verbal or numerical reasoning. In fact, their scores were average. What distinguished them was the sheer force of their personalities. Commenting on the research, Michael Dixon of the *Financial Times* observed: 'They shared a voracious need to have power over other people..... They were also marked by a lust for personal achievement, being fiercely competitive in pursuing the extremely high aims they had set for themselves to the extent of being ruthless with anyone seen as standing in their way.' But if that is all leadership amounts to, we are left looking for qualities which Machiavelli's Prince, or even Hitler, Al Capone or any other leading bandit embodied in abundance. This is the point at which loose talk on this vital combustible subject becomes dangerous.

Any serious attempt to analyse concepts of leadership raises a complex of issues, ranging from political and social values, from shareholder rights to citizenships, from the bottom line to top line of managerial responsibilities.

We are not managing in a vacuum. For instance, we are conditioned - willingly, I take it - by our commitments to democratic standards. Managers in a democracy have an awkward question to face daily: why should anyone obey an order? This question lies at the heart of managing any human group. Where is the point of sovereignty, the source of power? The question begs its way through our recorded history.

Any advanced democracy struggles with balancing of reconciling democracy and free markets. It is not an easy balance if it means a large number of democratic citizens are unemployed. It is neither easy nor inevitable. The rise of the economies of Asia/Pacific are providing competitive evidence that economic progress does not always have democracy as a corollary. Certainly for leaders in Western management, 'being ruthless with anyone seen as standing in the way' seems a short-term answer to the begging question.

### Lessons in command

In crisis, in war particularly, the answer is crudely simplified. As a raw recruit in the Second World War I found myself in the famous cartoon situation at dawn: on a massive expanse of parade ground I dropped my rifle. The Regimental Sergeant Major's voice exploded across the compound: 'Take his name, Sergeant!' 'Yessir.' As a fumbler with a rifle, I was left in no doubt about obedience. In fact, military experience gave me my first inklings of command. In my sphere of combat, there were extraordinary examples of leadership - Lord Mountbatten and Field-Marshal Slim.

Mountbatten's style of command was as daring as his strategies. He had the essentials of leadership beyond his sheer professionalism as a navy man. For a start, he had luck. During the Second World War, Mountbatten arrived in the Far East just as the Japanese were reaching the limit of their military expansion. The timing of his arrival was at a turning point. Then he also had the glamorous knack of dramatising the big decisions. He needed, for example, to achieve a fundamental change of attitude in the management of the south-east Asian Command. To achieve this he shipped his headquarters from Delhi to Kandy in (then) Ceylon. Moving headquarters is a move I have imitated and recommend to any manager trying to convert attitudes which have congealed into defeatism: buildings can smell of defeat and, literally, a change of view can help. (We under-rate the importance

of physical details of management in so many ways -
round tables, for example, do make a difference.)

But the most critical component in Mountbatten's leadership style was that he 'connected'. He took immense
trouble to connect with the people. They may have been
way down the line of command, but he realised he relied
on them to complete his mission effectively. I happened
to be a lowly member of a group he addressed before he
left Delhi. His news was disappointing. One of the
reasons that he, with his naval background, had been
made Supreme Commander in the south-east Asian
sphere of war was because a seaborne invasion of Burma
had been the objective: the global strategy of the Allies
switched priorities and landing-craft for his armies had
been requisitioned for use in Italy. Yet, he described all
this with a dash, a direct and practised charm. As pep
talks went (and we had quite enough regularly to be able
to judge) Mountbatten's was a masterly performance -
indeed, he was a performer, an actor-manager, who
played the Black Prince superbly.

Field-Marshal Slim cast his spells quite differently. He
didn't have the handsome charisma of Mountbatten.
When I heard him give us a pep-talk he was hefty, loosely
dressed in baggy shirts and shorts, with a wide-brimmed
hat and a tall stick. He created confidence and enthusiasm by daring to share his problems. He levelled with us.
Above all, he took the trouble to be there, among his
troops, even if they were in the middle of the jungle.

33

While personality remains a mystery, 'being there' seems to me the stuff of leadership at every level of managing. Shakespeare's Ulysses, in *Troilus and Cressida,* puts it beautifully: 'When that the general is not like the hive to whom the foragers do all repair, what honey is expected?'

### Establishing legitimacy to lead

Of course, war and even Cold War, make life dramatically simple. In business the parameters of leadership are less clear. There are no King's or Queen's Regulations to hold the line; there are no Regimental Sergeant-Majors with booming voices to put the inefficient on a charge. Managerial power is also fundamentally a contrast to uniformed power. And to political power - managers are not elected by those they manage; they can make no claim to the sovereignty of the people. While there may be many lords in the boardrooms, only very few claim a divine right of management.

As a result, management has continually to establish - and re-establish - its own legitimacy to lead. It has to justify its actions and decisions to an increasingly disparate body of what is now fashionably labelled 'stakeholders' - shareholders, employees, the local community, the City, financial analysts, media and pressure groups.

And when the stakeholders assess management, the quality of the leadership is increasingly decisive. It is right, it should be so. I resist strongly the dichotomy sometimes made between management and leading.

Managing means leading, making things happen through people. That is relevant at every level of management, not just the profiled personalities at the top. Over a generation I have seen the awareness grow: diffused leadership in an organisation means teamwork. Immediately after the war, the word 'leader' was highly unattractive: it had a sinister echo of the Fuhrer principle. Brecht summed it all up in his characteristically sour wit: 'Pity the land that needs a hero.'

Nowadays, leadership is deodorised. There are leadership training courses; leadership forums even (a touch paradoxical for those who think of leaders as rugged individuals). So we are all challenged to declare ourselves on this priority.

## Leadership in three dimensions

For my part, I have always regarded management as leadership in three dimensions: economic, entrepreneurial and social.

The economic dimension is instantly recognisable: it includes the professional process of combining commerce, administration and technical skills, towards profitable objectives. A leader has to know the basics of his or her craft. The entrepreneurial side is far more difficult to measure, but what is measurable in management is seldom all there is to measure, and is not always the most important. There is an area of imagination and energy, of risk-taking and of risk-making, of seizing the changes which others do not seize, of seeing ahead and somehow shaping the future, letting it have your way. It is an ill-defined, but well-established element of success. And I reckon we can all of us recognise a real entrepreneur at 300 yards on a misty day.

In the social dimension, managers and organisations are far less self-assured. The role of business managers in co-ordinating the culture of their enterprise and that of the community is rapidly emerging. The trouble is that these two forces do not necessarily thrust in the same direction. We have to explore this social dimension much more confidently. Increasingly, managers will have to become capable of interpreting and communicating their business objectives in ways that make sense in social terms. The board agenda of any sizeable company in the 1990s and beyond will not be able to leave social policy hopefully under 'any other business'. Whatever the politics of Maastricht and the Social Chapter, the reality of the need to reconcile management's methods and its economic purposes with those of the community within which it works will not go away. The concept of the economic company may well seem as dead and skeletal to the next generation as the economic man in our own.

If, as we are often entreated to do, we are to learn lessons from the Japanese, we should realise that, above all, their success (so far) has depended on the quality of its socially-minded management in partnership with government.  Consensus in Thatcher's administration was anathema.  The Japanese wallow in it and come up smelling of roses.  This seems relatively effortless for the Japanese.  Their enterprise seems to have grown up naturally in this third dimension, with business and community working if not always in unison, then in harmony.

A manager's success in fusing all three dimensions depends on his or her capacity to lead.  The truth is that people prefer being *led* to being *managed*.  The process of good leadership makes a leader realise how much depends on others.  The leader has to listen to a myriad of different viewpoints, opinions, aspirations and grievances.  To do so, leaders have to be accessible - not on an occasional basis, but continually they have to 'be there'.

## *Leadership for the future*

In fusing the differing dimensions together, the leaders of the future will:

- ◆ **take risks and be professional** - they may be qualified through an MBA or some other business degree, or through sheer experience.  They will be professional and yet be entrepreneurial in their willingness to take risks.

- ◆ **educate and build teams** - they will champion and create learning organisations.  Amid the enthusiasm for management development programmes too much of what managers have been trained in has been force-fed. The essential challenge for managers to develop themselves must be carefully preserved and nurtured. Personal responsibility must not be swept aside in tides of enthusiasm for cloning the good organisation man or woman. The temptation for senior managers is to shape younger managers in their own image, to create a self-perpetuating tradition of what you need to be like and what skills you must have to succeed in a particular organisation. Responsibility is the best teacher and the best leaders are those who can entrust people with true responsibility.

38

♦ **be international in experience, practice and outlook.** Management and business is now truly international. Its leaders must set the pace of the process of internationalisation.

♦ **be political animals** - they will be interested in the efficiency of government and in creating a mutually supportive relationship between government (not politicians) and the business world.

♦ **be citizens** - they will share concerns with the community as a whole, such as the social priorities of the environment and unemployment.

And, with all, they will require that essential luck. Napoleon always asked if his prospective generals were lucky - this is well known, but Napoleon also estimated that the luck of a general could only last six years. I spent

seven years as chairman of BR and appreciate the senti-
ment. For the modern business leader this is an important
lesson. Staying with an organisation or in a particular
job for too long can diminish what made the leader
successful in the first place. You find yourself losing time
in defensive talk over past decisions, especially the wrong
ones. You lose impetus, look over your shoulder too
often, reflecting not renewing, repeating and not refreshing,
stroking and not spurring on, purring and not prodding
yourself. So, without really noticing, the energy, the
nerve and direction dissipate. The time inevitably comes
in the career of any leader when you have to allow others
the opportunity to take the organisation forward.

For the potential leaders of tomorrow, this is a demanding list. Only a paragon could manage to juggle all these
priorities. With luck and good humour, some might
manage not to drop all the balls at once, and if they all
fall, at least see where they land. This is an ideal manager,
one I have never met, though I have met managers with
ideals as well as success.

Sceptics may argue that such idealistic notions forget or
conveniently overlook the importance of the bottom-
line. The bottom-line remains of vital importance, but
as we move towards the next century, there is also a
top-line for managers. They will have to look beyond
the values of shareholders. Already the great international
corporations are having to define their social values
clearly, in terms of the environment, quality of life and a
sense of fairness of opportunity.

The life of a leader is no longer simple, if it ever truly was. Leaders have to see the challenge from the point of view of the employee, the citizen in society. 'And when we think we lead, we are most led,' remarked Byron. The employee asks the fundamental, simple questions: what is expected of me; how am I doing; what do I do to get ahead; where, if things go wrong, is justice; who really cares; is what I do worthwhile; am I meaningful? Business leaders have a duty to listen if they are to perform their jobs well and if they are to synthesise the three dimensions of management.

On a day-to-day level there is a ready stream of answers to these simple questions. People do what they are told because of pay or persuasion, fear or faith, greed or duty, honour or glory, lust for power or simply love. A manager tries to magically blend all these reasons together through leadership. But, at another deeper level, there is less clarity, more significance, more mystery. We obey or conform, or not, for reasons, which as individuals we may not be able, or even want, to explain. Our motives are as unique to us as our fingerprints. The philosophy of management begins where any belief starts, at some truly unfathomable depth of being where, like buried treasure, lies the ultimate question of the meaning of life, It is our response to that question that give meaning to our work and to our giving and taking of orders.

# SIR PETER INGE

*On Leadership*

---

*Field Marshal Sir Peter Inge* GCB CIMgt *is Chief of the Defence Staff.*

After studying at the Royal Military Academy at Sandhurst he was commissioned to the Green Howards in 1956.  During a distinguished army career he has served in Hong Kong, Malaya, Germany, Libya and the UK.

I am in a profession where leadership is fundamentally important to success. Yet, even after a career of over 30 years in the armed services, it is always embarrassing as an individual to talk or write about leadership. If you theorise or generalise about leadership there is the suspicion that people will think that you regard yourself as a great leader. Leadership is so personal, so special and so elusive a talent that people should always be very wary of assuming that they have that great gift.

In fact, much of my inspiration and thoughts about leadership are drawn from meeting, listening to and reading the writings of Field Marshal Viscount Slim (1891-1970). Like many great leaders, Field Marshal Slim had an immense presence. I recently listened again to a talk he gave on leadership to my Staff College course in 1966. It remained inspirational. The Field Marshal could talk about leadership from a highly practical perspective: he was a famously successful practitioner as well as a thinker. Under his leadership, the 14th Army which consisted of soldiers from many nations, fought a memorable campaign to recapture Burma from the Japanese in the Second World War. He led them 'from defeat into victory'.[1] Not only was the Field Marshal an outstanding leader in his own right but he also thought deeply about the subject and his book, *Defeat Into Victory* is one of the finest, if not the finest, General's book of World War Two. In particular his analysis of the foundations of morale is the best I have ever read.

Clearly, there are a number of characteristics and qualities of a leader which are important for leaders in all
walks of life and not just those in the armed services. The
fundamental question in the opinion of Field Marshal
Slim, and I think most other leaders, is courage, and he
is talking about moral as well as physical courage. In
particular, he thought moral courage was the fundamental quality of great leadership.

Moral courage involves having the strength to act
through your own convictions and to face up to your own
shortcomings. While people with moral courage frequently have physical courage as well, there is a limit to
any one person's reservoir of physical stamina, strength
and bravery. At times people will need to recharge their
batteries in order to ensure that they do not overdraw
their bank balance of physical courage. In contrast, the
more you use your moral courage the easier it becomes
to use and, of course, the reverse is equally true - if you
fail to exercise moral courage it will become increasingly
more difficult to do so and particularly over major issues.

## Tests of moral courage

While moral courage may suggest grave and momen-
tous situations, in practice it can involve apparently minor events. As a young officer you find yourself facing
30 soldiers who are suddenly under your command. It
is quite a test. They are, you find out, marvellous people
often with strong and sometimes difficult personalities.

They inevitably continue to provide challenges to your moral courage. If someone with a strong personality has a dirty rifle you face a test of moral courage - do you ignore it in an effort to avoid his disapproval or do you reprimand him and face the difficulties this creates?

This lesson was very effectively taught to me early in my career by my first Regimental Sergeant Major, who had won a marvellous DCM in the Normandy campaign. When I saw him in the distance I did all I could to disappear. However, on one occasion I had to sit next to him when I visited the Sergeant's Mess as Orderly Officer. He said that he had noticed that a solider had failed to salute me earlier in the day and that I had failed to speak to him. He said that he did not mind the fact that the soldier had not saluted. What mattered much more was the fact that I had noticed and failed to do anything about it. If I did not exercise discipline in barracks then I was even more likely to fail to exercise it on operations. It was a salutary lesson, and I believe it brings out very clearly that if you ignore apparently trivial matters then you will find it difficult to exert your moral courage in more demanding circumstances.

Clearly, knowledge is an important part of leadership, although the knowledge required by a young Platoon Commander is very different, of course, to that required of a Corps Commander. Yet the Corps Commander in addition to knowing his trade at that level, must still retain enough general knowledge of his command, and what it is capable of doing, in order that when he goes to visit the servicemen and servicewomen he is able to discuss with them the key issues which concern them.   Related to this, of course, is the importance of being able to communicate, which is a vital prerequisite for any leader.

'I learnt...that one did not need to be an orator to be effective,' wrote Field Marshal Slim.  'Two things were necessary: first to know what you were talking about, and second and most important, to believe it yourself.  I found that if one kept the bulk of one's talk to the material things that men were interested in, food, pay, leave, beer, mail, and the progress of operations, it was safe to end on a higher note - the spiritual foundations - and I always did.'

So communication is very important to leadership, but you do not have to be an extrovert or a great orator to succeed as a leader - you do have to be able to tell it as it is.   A good communicator will have the advantage of being able to project his personality thus helping to inspire confidence.   So the Armed Services remains a melting pot for leaders, it places young men and young women in tense situations where there can be a very real and imminent threat to life, perhaps to their own life and to those they command.  It demands judgement, coolness and maturity.  A patrol in Bosnia, in the air, on the sea or on the ground may face a crisis at any moment; this is the stark day-to-day operational reality.  In a tight situation people look for leadership and they require to be led.

This is why tough, demanding and realistic training is fundamentally important for all fighting services and if we cut corners with it in peace time, we will be in danger of failure on operations.

Training can provide important lessons for leaders at all levels. I can remember to this day when I was a Platoon Commander on a major exercise for the Battalion in Hong Kong. My Platoon Sergeant, Sergeant Gash, came to tell me that one of the sections was in bad order and needed sorting out. I asked him to go and do just that. He said no, I should go and sort it out because then the Section Commander would know that I was not prepared to accept second best and more importantly I would know Sergeant Gash was not prepared to accept second best. I believe such lessons remain with you for the rest of your life.

## In search of ethos

Central also to leadership must be a willingness to allow people to make mistakes to encourage their development and to learn from those mistakes. This requires flexibility. Although the great leaders, such as Slim and Montgomery, were notable for their willpower, they also never allowed it to become blind stubbornness.

So, the leader must understand those he is responsible for as people and individuals. My first Company Sergeant Major, Company Sergeant Major Read, quizzed me after muster parade about a particular soldier in my platoon.

It was always a different one. After about a week I plucked up courage to ask him why. He replied: 'I have been watching you sir, you are very good at inspecting their boots, anklets, belts, cap badge, etc, but you don't look them in the eye. You need to get to those 30 eyes sir, because if you lead them on operations you will know when they are under pressure, frightened or need special attention.' I asked him why he didn't give me that advice at the start of my tour as a Platoon Commander. He replied: 'You would have soon forgotten it, but now you will never forget.'

I also believe that the human side of leadership, certainly in the armed forces, must contain a strong element of what I call ethos. It is something which is difficult to talk about but it is the sort of spirit that motivates armed forces and is very much part of what makes people put their lives on the line. It is certainly not a policy, nor a science, it is a mixture of emotional, intellectual and moral qualities. It is about comradeship and team spirit; it is about integrity and the high quality of people one is fortunate to work and serve with and I emphasise the word serve because I believe that although monetary reward is important, it is not a driving force.

Ethos is also about tradition, but I do not mean the wrong sort of old fashioned tradition, the one which recognises the importance that human beings attach to a sense of continuity, familiarity and pride in the institution in which he or she lives and works. I recently saw a

wonderful quote: 'We must not allow the ethos or ethic
of service to be replaced by the culture of the contract
and we must not allow the pearl of leadership to be
replaced by the metal of management.'   Please do no
think that I am denigrating management, but I believe
that man management is a facet of leadership.

In 1942, addressing his officers in Africa for the first
time, Field Marshal Montgomery observed: 'I believe that
one of the first duties of a commander is to create what I
call "atmosphere"; and in that atmosphere, his staff,
subordinate commanders and troops will live and work
and fight.'   From that moment Montgomery began estab-
lishing his own unique 'atmosphere'.   I think there is a
linkage between my conception of ethos and Field Marshal Montgomery's atmosphere.   I think all organisations need an emotional spark of ethos.

In *Defeat Into Victory*, Field Marshal Slim described his
thoughts on this indefinable aspect of leadership:

> '*Morale is a state of mind.   It is that intangible force*
> *which will move a whole group of men to give their*
> *last ounce to achieve something, without counting*
> *the cost to themselves; that makes them feel they*
> *are part of something greater than themselves.   If*
> *they are to feel that, their morale must, if it is to*
> *endure - and the essence of morale is that it should*
> *endure - have certain foundations.   These founda-*
> *tions are spiritual, intellectual, and material, and*
> *that is the order of their importance.   Spiritual first,*

*because only spiritual foundations can stand real strain. Next intellectual, because men are swayed by reason as well as feeling. Material last - important, but last - because the highest kinds of morale are often met when material conditions are lowest.'*

Leadership is intensely personal and it has to remain open to individual interpretations. Some officers I have known break many of the basic rules of leadership and yet they have a spark that ignites something in their soldiers who follow them willingly.

49

In the armed services, as I suspect in the business world, traditional concepts and understanding of what constitutes leadership have undergone a thorough process of re-examination. At the time when I joined the army as a national serviceman only three people of 20 private soldiers wanted to become regulars; and I wasn't one of them. Yet, in that barrack room, a wonderful esprit de corps developed even though we accepted things without them being explained to us. I don't believe that would work today.

## Building on the fundamentals

Leaders nowadays in all walks of life explain the thinking behind decisions and the various options a great deal more than we once did. I don't believe this in any way undermines the fundamentals of leadership and discipline, and indeed it should enhance them. The fundamentals remain in place, but they have been adapted to fit into the practices and expectations of rather different and somewhat demanding times. In addition, the style of leadership, say for a company commander, is going to be very different to that of an Army Group Commander and it will be different again in departments of state like the Ministry of Defence, but one should never forget that people, wherever they are, still require and deserve leadership. Different techniques work for different people, so the leader has to be pragmatic and flexible, but I still believe that the fundamentals remain.

In the armed forces we are dealing with more intelligent and better educated people than ever before. People now are extremely professional and study and take their profession seriously. They have a more outward view, ask more questions and challenge conventions and accepted practices. It can feel as if they are the young Turks and we are the reactionaries. Understandably, there is a desire to practise a greater degree of consensus than perhaps was previously the case. Even so, there has to be a balance. It can't all be consensus, but equally nor can leadership be based simply on shouting louder. Trust has to be developed so that instant decisions can be made and obeyed by others.

The fact that leadership, like other forms of behaviour, continually evolves is a healthy thing. You don't find static leaders. They, too, move and develop to fit changing circumstances. To do so requires enormous self-awareness and self-discipline. The latter is a critical factor in the armed forces where the emphasis is not, as many believe, on enforced discipline, although that has a part, but on self-discipline.

We put incredible demands on our leaders. One minute we send our armed servicemen and women to the Gulf to challenge a dictator and the next they are peace keeping in Northern Ireland or Bosnia, both of which are very different. They and their leaders have to be immensely versatile.

Leadership is as important now as it has ever been, and is necessary in all levels of an organisation. Undoubtedly certain changes mean that leadership has become more difficult and complex and is more in the public gaze. However, perhaps great leaders will continue to exercise these challenges through their moral courage.

*References*

1. Field Marshal Slim's book, *Defeat Into Victory* (Castle & Co, 1956)

# SIR COLIN MARSHALL

## On Leadership

---

*Sir Colin Marshall is chairman of British Airways.*

Sir Colin began his career as a cadet purser with the Orient Steam Navigation Company. In 1958 he joined the Hertz Corporation as a management trainee based in Chicago. He was then appointed general manager of Hertz's Mexican operations before becoming assistant to the company president in New York. In 1961 he returned to the UK to run Hertz's operations in the UK, the Netherlands and Belgium.

Sir Colin then joined Avis, becoming vice president and regional manager for Europe and, in 1971, executive vice president and chief operating officer. In 1975 he became president of Avis and later chief executive officer.

After a short period with Sears, Sir Colin was appointed chief executive of British Airways in 1983, forging a notable partnership with the then chairman, Lord King. In 1989 he became deputy chairman and, in 1993 chairman. He is also a director of Grand Metropolitan, HSBC Holdings, US Air and IBM UK, as well as being involved in a wide range of other bodies.

Leadership is an amalgam of many different facets - vision, dedication and drive - and an array of others. They are rarely found in one person. Yet, while the individual characteristics of a leader vary from person to person, there are common foundations: you have to be respected by those you are going to lead; you need to be a good communicator, willing and able to stand at the front of the organisation; and people must be prepared to follow you.

54

There is nothing revolutionary in this. Leadership and management are in many respects the application of common sense, though this needs to be combined with humility and a willingness to recognise your own fallibility and that of others. Good leaders acknowledge their mistakes.

I believe that leaders aren't simply born with innate leadership skills which are waiting to be discovered, but that leaders can be developed. Indeed, there are more opportunities than ever before for young managers to enhance their knowledge of leadership and develop their practical leadership skills. In the 1950s, when I began my working life as a cadet purser with the Orient Steam Navigation Company, leadership was not a subject to be studied formally. But experience was something which was there to be acquired. Travelling the seas of the world was a great experience in meeting people, exposing myself to the wealth of political, cultural and human difference.

I have been very fortunate in how my career has developed. I was in the right place at the right time. But it is not all down to luck. Luck goes with success. Since 1959 when I was given the chance to run Hertz's operations in Mexico I have been running my own show. Hertz gave me tremendous responsibilities at a very early stage in my career. This combination of trust and independence proved critical in my development.

## Opportunities and inspirations

At Hertz I worked for Donald Petrie who has proved a life-long influence on my ideas about management and leadership. He was the first person I worked for in the United States. In 1958 he offered me a job as his PA. I emigrated to the US, went to work for Hertz in Chicago and never expected to return to the UK.

Don was a lawyer by background and a deep thinker. He had strategic vision and was good at application, a rare combination. I worked directly for him only for six months in Chicago and was then, in 1959, asked to go to Mexico at short notice and take over Hertz's operations there. At the end of 1960 Don was elected as president of Hertz and contacted me in Mexico, asking me to come to work for him as his assistant in New York. It was a tremendous opening. I accepted and prepared to move to New York. By the time I arrived there had been a managerial revolution. I cooled my heels and was then offered a job in London. I seized the opportunity.

Later Petrie joined with Robert Townsend (who wrote the bestseller *Up the Organisation*) in taking leadership control of the rather moribund Avis. Don was chairman of the executive committee and Townsend was chief executive.

After spending three periods of my working life in the United States, my business inspiration remains American. Alongside Don Petrie, perhaps the most influential figure for me was Harold Geneen, the legendary leader of ITT. Geneen's style and imprint had a decisive influence on the development of my thinking about management and how to run a worldwide organisation. 'You read a book from the beginning to end. You run a business the opposite way. You start with the end, and then you do everything you must to reach it,' Geneen commented.

Under Geneen, ITT turned in remarkable financial results year after year through rigorous financial controls and a continuous stream of acquisitions. He proclaimed his aim of achieving 10 per cent profit growth every single year - and actually managed to record profit gains for 58 successive quarters.

Geneen became president and chief executive of ITT in 1959. At the time, the company had poor profit margins and was dependent on overseas earnings. With Geneen at its helm, ITT bought, merged or acquired 350 companies and, when he retired, it was a $22 billion giant with 375,000 employees.

ITT acquired Avis when I was new to the organisation running the European end of the business. Geneen was a remarkable man. Every month there were management meetings in New York and Brussels which gathered together the chief executives from all of ITT's operations in a particular continent. They lasted all day and, often, well into the night.

It is difficult to be inspired by people you haven't worked with. Not many business people are particularly well-known. Beyond the business community I have drawn inspiration from the likes of Margaret Thatcher - the privatisation of BA was, after all, one of the key events in my life - and Churchill.

After a brief spell with Sears, I joined BA in February 1983. At this time, before privatisation, the company was performing badly. In 1981 its losses were £69.9 million. The entire ethos and focus of the organisation was wrong. The concentration was on operations, running planes efficiently so that passengers completed their journeys safely and on time. These elements are vital, but fundamental changes were clearly required. Bureaucracy still permeated the organisation. It was slow moving and risk-averse. While the public sector is concerned with eliminating risk, managing in the private sector is focused on reducing risk to an acceptable degree.

Leadership is about a commitment to people. Before and since privatisation in 1987, BA has set about revolutionising its attitudes to people - inside and outside the company.

## Objectives for change

Over the months following my arrival, a set of corporate objectives were developed which pinned the company's future on the development of service excellence throughout its operations. The seven central objectives identified were:

- ◆ to provide the highest levels of service to all customers, passengers, shippers, travel agents and freight agents

- ◆ to preserve high professional and technical standards in order to achieve the highest levels of safety

- ◆ to provide a uniform image worldwide and to maintain a specific set of standards for each clearly defined market segment

- ◆ to respond quickly and sensitively to the changing needs of our present and potential customers

- ◆ to maintain and, where opportunity occurs, expand our present route structure

- ◆ to manage, operate and market the airline in the most efficient manner

- ◆ to create a service and people-oriented work environment, assuring all employees of fair pay and working conditions and continuing concern for their career.

Research showed that two thirds of recent airline passengers thought that BA was neither better nor worse than other airlines. While this was not exactly a ringing endorsement, it also presented an opportunity for BA to achieve a vital competitive edge through service. Neutral responses could be turned into positive experiences and support.

The first step was the staff awareness programme, 'Putting People First'. This programme, launched at the end of 1983, was initially aimed at the 15,000 people in direct contact with customers. Its success was such that it was extended throughout the airline. Initially it was criticised by some as being too American - though in fact it was developed in the UK by a Danish company. The programme lasted two days and the groups were up to 180 strong. I made a point of closing as many of the programme's seminars as I could. They ran for two and a half years and I closed 40 per cent of them.

I was conscious when we embarked on the programme that it couldn't be a one-off. It had to re-focus the organisation, changing it from a company focused on operations to one which was led by the marketplace and one which recognised the needs of customers. I thought it would take at least five years, but more likely a decade to really carry it through. To achieve genuine culture change takes time, effort and the overriding concern to get at the values involved. The reason so many companies seem to achieve a useful change in culture and then slowly disintegrate over the passage of even short spans of time is that one suspects they confuse the appearance of culture change, the presence of the symbols, with the needed solid change in values and their acceptance.

## Leading change

Clearly, achieving a major transformation in any organisation requires leadership. Change at companies such as ICI, General Electric and Xerox has revolved round strong leaders such as John Harvey-Jones, Jack Welch and, at Xerox, David Kearns. Indeed, work by Harvard Business School's John Kotter has identified eight steps in the process of leading change:

1. a leader with a good track record is appointed

2. one with an outsider's openness to new ideas

3. who creates a sense of crisis

4. who creates and communicates a new vision and new strategies

5. who then behaves accordingly, acting as a role model

6. and thus involves others in key jobs in the drive for change

7. these others then use thousands of opportunities to influence behaviour throughout the organisation

8.  producing tangible results within two years, thus reinforcing the drive to persevere without the change programme.

Putting People First was only the beginning for BA. It was accompanied by 'Managing People First' which focused on how to lead, to be willing to take risks and raise your head above the parapet. This one-week training programme aimed to help managers deal with the transition and to manage their people through the process of change.

We have now completed the fourth of the total employee programmes. The second, entitled 'A Day in the Life', focused on what the company actually does in its day-to-day operations. Employees wanted to know about their own company so we put together a programme including snapshots of eight departments.

The third programme, 'To be the Best', focused on the competition in world markets and the fourth, 'Winners', on quality and customer service. A fifth is now being developed to be launched in 1996.

Some observers and the media regularly express a degree of scepticism about such programmes, as if they are window-dressing. They are not. All feature a closing slot from senior directors to demonstrate how important we think they are. Crucial to the entire process is a breaking down of barriers and an opening of lines of communication. People are invited to write down questions during the seminars and at the end we answer them. People at the top of the organisational hierarchy must have access to people in the workplace. If they don't they quickly become cut off.

Communication is a vital part of the leadership role. I get around the organisation. I talk to engineers in the hangars, pilots and crew on the planes and customers. If a member of the cabin crew tells me that one of the passengers isn't happy I talk to him or her.

If people believe in the organisation and what it is doing they will achieve their potential, as well as helping the business to achieve its. When BA was floated, 94 per cent of staff took the opportunity to buy shares in the company.

## High profile partners

Throughout these changes my relationship with the then chairman, Lord King, was highly important - the chairman-chief executive relationship should be one of the most vital in any business. While Lord King dealt with the public side of the business I concentrated on the industry relationships critical to our development. The divide between our jobs was clear and, most importantly, it worked. I was left to run the company while Lord King fulfilled the role of chairman working closely with the board, and taking on a wider public role dealing with public relations and government relations. At that time, immediately after privatisation, the political element was high on the agenda - though our business, like telecommunications, is permanently embroiled in politics.

Away from this high profile public role, Lord King served as a sounding board to me as chief executive and to other senior managers. Such a sounding board is one of the great things any chief executive must have - and is a role I increasingly try to take on myself. As a chief executive you can become isolated and lonely. You need to constantly guard against this happening.

The problem commonly encountered by leaders - in whatever field - is that the length of time they have spent in office leads to them being cut off from reality. As a result, they fail to recognise their faults and mistakes. Leaders have to be wary of longevity. Robert Townsend, for example, is a fervent believer that no-one should be in one position for more than five years. I don't subscribe to that view and believe that it depends entirely on the individual. Even so, you must watch for signs of egotism and a lack of willingness to acknowledge mistakes.

No leader should become distant from the people actually doing the day-to-day work. Unless a leader is people-oriented he or she will not understand the people they are leading. While different leaders are required for different situations, all must concentrate heavily on opening up communications.

As chairman of British Airways I am in a position where leadership is required, indeed it is expected from me.

That is how I am perceived and how I see myself. I relish it and believe that if you don't enjoy something you should stop doing it - there was only one job I didn't enjoy and I got out of it within 18 months.

The role of leadership is especially important in a service business. If morale is low then you simply can't deliver customer service. That is what a service business is all about. Leaders inspire an organisation and take responsibility for creating the essential motivation to move things forward, constantly improve and meet objectives. Excellence in leadership is a prerequisite for business success.

# VALERIE STRACHAN

*On Leadership*

---

*Valerie Strachan* CB *has been chairman of the Board of Customs and Excise since 1993. She was previously deputy chairman from 1987 until 1993.*

She joined Customs and Excise in 1961 after studying at Manchester University. Her civil service career has included working in a variety of departments including the Department of Economic Affairs, the Home Office and the Treasury. She headed the Treasury and Cabinet Office's Joint Management Unit between 1985 and 1987.

Leadership is the quality we all hope to find in those who are in some way 'in charge', whether in the private or the public sector. A real leader, I think, is easy to recognise. He or she is the one who guesses the future right, who can see what is needed to keep the organisation going - and going forward - and who can, most importantly, convince everyone in the organisation to follow his or her lead. While such skills are easy to recognise, they are notoriously difficult to achieve.

My experience of observing and practising leadership has been exclusively within the civil service, and mainly within HM Customs and Excise. Increasingly, public and private sector leadership skills and styles appear to be converging. Yet, there remain many unique features about leading a civil service organisation.

First, a civil service department is carrying out the policies of the Government. The head of the department (unlike the head of a company) doesn't have the option of deciding what business the company should be in, or what activities to drop. Nor does the head of the department have a completely free hand in deciding how to manage the department: he or she has to operate within a framework of rules and guidelines. And, particularly in recent years, the Government has had definite policies about the management of the public sector. A range of changes, initiatives and programmes - such as the Financial Management Initiative, Next Steps and market testing - have had repercussions on the way the civil service is managed and led.

There are other important differences in practising leadership in public service rather than in the private sector. One is the nature of the uncertainties the head of department faces in guessing the future. The head of a private sector company has to guess at what the market is going to want in the medium term: the market consisting of all the actual and potential customers in the world. Along the way, he or she has to gauge population movements, government changes, exchange rate fluctuations, commodity prices, taxation regimes, and a growing array of other factors. In effect, there is an entire series of large-scale, but essentially impersonal, influences. My guess is that it would be relatively unusual for the head of a private sector company to have to try to forecast the likely wishes of a small number of individuals. In contrast, that is exactly what a civil service permanent secretary has to do.

In managing a department, the biggest influences are the requirements, aspirations and expectations of ministers. You might think that the permanent secretary has the smooth end of the lollipop compared with the head of a company. After all, he or she knows the ministers, and it is part of the job to understand what they want and, as far as possible, deliver it to them. It appears straightforward but, while the permanent secretary certainly should know what the current minister wants, he or she has to consider whether the minister is likely to be overruled by the Treasury, or by the Prime Minister. The capable permanent secretary knows the game well enough to be able to make a sensible judgement.

However, no matter how sensible the judgement, history repeatedly proves that any minister can be removed by an accident of political fate. What about the next reshuffle? The next election? What will the next, unknown minister want? It can never be forgotten that a minister who knows what he or she wants should and will almost certainly get it - whatever 'it' may turn out to be.

As a result, the permanent secretary who is trying to exercise leadership has to remember that they are doing so under clear and certain restraints. They are leaders, but they are on a lead. It may be a very long lead - but the lead can be tugged or drastically shortened, at any time, either because the political personalities or because the political priorities have changed.

This might sound like a rather lengthy excuse for not trying to exercise leadership in the civil service. It is not and must not be. Civil servants are not unique in having to manage in conditions of uncertainty. But, the nature of the uncertainty is clearly and substantially different. Civil servants need leadership just like any other employees. In the case of my department, the commissioners of Customs and Excise, like the Board of Inland Revenue, have a statutory existence (unlike most civil service departments). We have a statutory responsibility for the care and management of customs and excise duties and VAT. We are also statutorily responsible for the enforcement of import and export prohibitions and restrictions. The very nature of these functions means that the department's leadership role has been less ambiguous than that in most other departments.

## The individual leader in public service

Leadership in the public sector takes place in a unique environment, but one which is influenced by the functions of departments and those who lead them. In the civil service, as elsewhere, leadership is a human science.

One of the most interesting developments I have observed in over 30 years as a civil servant has been the change in the way that heads of department have led their organisations. At the beginning of my career in the early 1960s, chairmen of Customs and Excise were very grand and remote individuals. There was no question of photographs of them appearing in annual reports; nor of messages being sent to all their staff. Even if you worked in the same building as the chairman, you might well not have known either what he looked like or how he behaved.

Though they appear distant and aloof to modern eyes, they were undoubtedly exercising leadership, in the sense that they exercised decisive influence to secure important objectives. But mass communication within the department was certainly not part of the process. This meant that my awareness of leadership depended entirely on how close I was to the centre of the action. I suspect that this rule applied throughout the civil service.

Reorganising Customs and Excise at the beginning of the 1970s, for example, was undoubtedly driven by the then chairman, Sir Wilfred Morton. From my perspective, however, the person I saw as leading the change at the time was not Sir Wilfred, but the assistant secretary in charge of negotiating with Staff Side, Angus Fraser, who became chairman several years later. To me an assistant secretary appeared to be an extremely important person.

The next year, I became part of the team which was preparing for the introduction of VAT. There was no doubt, in that case, that the lead was being taken by the then deputy chairman, Ronald Radford (again, a future chairman). He drove it very definitely (team members of the time still have extremely vivid memories of that!) and successfully, but he did it in the classic civil service way of the time - communication was mostly on paper and mostly channelled through his under secretaries.

All that was more than twenty years ago, and methods of exercising leadership have changed enormously over that period. A key feature has been the greater explicitness of the objectives set for the department. Historically, the chairman's objectives were not necessarily made explicit. But gradually this has changed. In 1981, for example, I was the commissioner in charge of collecting VAT. The civil service unions had entered into a dispute with the Government about pay. They had chosen the VAT computer as a selective target for industrial action, and from the first day of the strike the normal payment routine ground to a halt. On day one, the chairman, Sir Douglas Lovelock, put out a message, which I can vividly remember almost word for word: 'VAT isn't the unions' money; it isn't our money; it's the nation's money. It is the commissioners' duty to collect it and pay it into the Exchequer, and that is what we are going to try to do'. The dispute, in the event, dragged on for five months. It was certainly not the most enjoyable period of my career, but even now I find it hard to remember as clear a communication by a chairman of what he expected his colleagues to do, and why.

That was a very clearly defined objective. Now, my department has a clear framework of resources and objectives, and this year I expect to reach a management by outputs agreement with 'my' Treasury minister (currently the Paymaster General). So ministers and my staff alike expect me to lead, and be seen to lead, Customs and Excise. That expectation is reinforced by increasing media interest in senior civil servants. My predecessors, up till very recently, would have been astounded to see their names in the papers. For me it is part of the job.

*Managing change*

The biggest demand on leadership, of course, comes from the management of change. This is one feature which is unquestionably common to every contemporary organisation. When I took up my present job two years

71

ago, Customs and Excise had been through what felt like enormous changes over the previous few years. We had transformed into a department operating on Next Steps lines, with authority delegated so far as possible down the line; we had a new personnel management strategy; we had developed forward-looking strategies for all our main areas of work; and in preparing for the Single European Market had made big changes to just about all our operations. Other things being equal, it might have been nice to have a period of stability - especially since I do not believe in turning organisations upside down for the sake of it.

Other things were not, of course, equal. There were some further changes which I thought we needed to make. First, we are a law enforcement body; but I felt we needed to put more emphasis on helping people to comply with the law, rather than just taking vigorous action to prevent and detect non-compliance. Secondly, although we had a pretty good range of numerical performance measures for our effectiveness in collecting revenue and preventing drugs etc from being imported, we needed to improve the quality of how we did those things.

These were substantial shifts (though in a direction we had already started to go). And since they affected the way that thousands of individuals - customs officers, VAT officers, excise officers - approached their dealings with businesses and members of the public, it was essential that they were convinced of the reasons for the changes. That meant that managers throughout the department needed to be involved, and that we had to have answers to very reasonable questions, such as: 'How do I strike a balance between enforcing the law and being helpful to business?'

In addition, we were asked to carry out a Fundamental Expenditure Review. FER is the process which all departments are expected to undergo, to see whether their objectives remain valid, and whether there are different - and more cost effective - ways of achieving them. It was our turn in 1994.

For some departments, the FER has focused mainly on their programme expenditure, and the process has been driven by the departmental Minister. Customs had no programme expenditure - almost all our spending is on salaries, accommodation, and the capital equipment of our people. There were still political judgements to be made, but the main thrust of our review was about how we could perform the same tasks as before - collecting revenue, preventing drugs and other prohibited and restricted goods from entering or leaving the country - more efficiently and no less effectively.

In the event, my colleagues on the Board shaped and endorsed proposals which we believe *will* enable the department to deliver its objectives with fewer staff. While doing so, we had to satisfy colleagues within the department and outside that the proposals would work, that we would ensure that we had fallback positions if they turned out not to work as expected, and that we could manage the extremely difficult personnel implications (taking 4,000 staff out of an organisation of 25,000 people, even over five years, is never going to be simple). It has been my job to set out clearly for the dedicated and hard-working staff of the department what is going to happen, why it needs to happen, and how we are setting about it. It has meant a very big communications exercise, both internal and external. Above all, it has meant taking ownership of the exercise. If I did not make it clear that I believed in what we were doing, I could hardly expect managers and staff to implement the changes effectively. This seemed to me not the sort of situation where I could sensibly detach myself from the course of action which I was pursuing.

Having said all that, I have to keep remembering that this is all 'leadership on a lead'. The judgement that we can deliver our objectives just as effectively with fewer staff is one which I can make. But I also accept that any Government might set different objectives: for example, bring in *more* VAT (including *more* checking on ordinary businesses). If they do, then we will need to change course; because, after all, we are living in a democracy, in which I am the servant, not the elected representative.

The final point to re-emphasise is how leadership is exercised in a situation where authority is delegated down the line. Much of the change that we are now involved in - both those shifts in balance which I mentioned earlier and the FER changes - needs, not just the head of organisation setting the course, but managers and staff throughout the organisation understanding and accepting what is needed, and using their own initiative to achieve it. This means a carefully planned process, at each level from the Board downwards, of working out - and arguing out - the changes; then giving a lot of authority to managers to translate the requirements into what they are going to do; and then ensuring that the end results are achieved. It is more difficult to make change happen in an 'empowered' organisation; in many ways it demands more of the leader of the organisation to ensure that people are convinced of the right course, rather than just instructed; but I believe that, once people *are* convinced, the changes will be achieved far more effectively.

# Sir Raymond Lygo

*On Leadership*

---

*Sir Raymond Lygo KCB CIMgt is now chairman of Rutland Trust and TNT Europe and TNT Express (UK).*

His career began in 1938 when he started as a reading boy in a printing works with the aim of becoming an apprenticed compositor. He didn't. In 1940 he joined *The Times* as a messenger boy. Two years later Lygo joined the Royal Navy as a naval airman. An illustrious naval career led to him captaining HMS Ark Royal, becoming Vice Chief of Naval Staff and Chief of Naval Staff in 1978.

On leaving the navy, he joined British Aerospace, becoming managing director and then chief executive from 1986 until 1989.

It is curious how long it has taken for people to understand, if they yet do, the difference between management and leadership. The first point worth making, therefore, is that management is a purely mechanistic thing. It can be dealt with through balance sheets, as far as finance is concerned and through the management chain, as long as the organisation and manning of the structure is logical. In other words, you could almost place management in the hands of a computer to create the best network for the organisation, the most logical and straightforward structure, and the ratios and checks required to ensure that all is proceeding according to plan.

Leadership, on the other hand, derives its strength from the humanities. It is an exercise in inculcating the managerial process with humanity. As such, leadership stands alone but not separate from management. You can, of course, have excellent leadership qualities while not being a capable manager - hence the well known report on an officer which read 'his men will follow him anywhere, if only out of a sense of curiosity'.

Those of us who have served both in the armed forces and in industry and commerce will have experienced the very considerable variances between those different environments. Yet, I have found the experience of one very useful in coming to terms with the requirements of the other. On one occasion, when in command of my first Naval Air Squadron, I waited for a well-known fire-eating Admiral to descend on me from his large black RN car.

As he came out of the car he returned my salute and said 'What is most lacking in a naval officer's training, Lygo?'. 'Management training, sir', I said. 'Management!' he cried, looking at me in astonishment. 'Management, boy - leadership, leadership, that's what the Navy is all about. Management, I've never heard such nonsense'. At the time I ruminated, if he doesn't know the difference between leadership and management then we really are in trouble.

Later, addressing the IM for the first time, I suggested that its name should be changed to the Institute of Leadership. Leadership was, I argued, what was now needed - management already had too many text books written on it and if you hadn't learned about it there was something sadly wrong. I had also just become a Companion of the IM and pointed out that to dress ourselves up with titles which are supposed to depict our management experience was a nonsense and that the selection process by which we become so elevated should be a little stricter. In other words, the IM was not displaying good leadership.

## The leaders and the team

I was asked, soon after I joined British Aerospace, what were the major differences between the Navy and industry? Recognising it was a trick question, it was some time before I would allow myself to be drawn into a public reply but I soon got bored with waiting. 'I cannot make any comment about industry at large,' I said. 'But, as far as I see, the difference between the Navy and British Aerospace at the present time is that in the Services they are a slave to structure; succession planning is a thing that absorbs them because every two or three years, when the bell's struck, they all move round, so that if they didn't have decent succession planning they would be in chaos; and they spend most of their time training each other, endlessly training, because in peace time they have absolutely nothing else to do. Whereas in British Aerospace, I see no structure, no succession planning and nobody trains anybody for anything.' At the time this was not a great exaggeration.

The fact is that - whatever the organisation - people want to be part of a team and they also want to be successful. I have never known anyone who has said to me: 'I have no wish to be successful'. But, of course, you can measure success in many ways. It doesn't only have to be measured in promotions through the system. When trying to dissuade a young man who wished to leave the Navy, at a time when the engagement arrangements entrapped recruits into a kind of mediaeval servitude, a process which I later changed, he said after listening to me: 'It's all right for you, sir, you're a success'. I pointed to the gold stripes on my sleeve and said: 'Are you referring to these? Do these mean I am a success? I may be a success in the terms with which these gold stripes measure me, but am I a successful father, am I a successful husband, am I a successful or happy member of the community at large? Which are you going to settle for?

You could of course be all of these things, but you must have some sense of priority'. Therefore, motivating people to be satisfied with their lot, or at least enthusiastic members of a team, has to take into account all aspects of their employment and ambition.

Many years ago during the war, I was walking along a passageway in a large aircraft carrier when the Commander, a man I respected enormously, stopped in his tracks and looked after a rating who had passed him and was coming towards me. As I caught up with the Commander he said: 'I don't known what this Navy is coming to, Lygo. Do you know what that man just said to me?' 'No, sir' said I. 'He said "Good morning, Commander"'. At that time to speak to an officer when not being spoken to was considered to be just not done. In his Navy he might have been right, but I was to spend the rest of my 36 years in the Navy trying to get my men to say: 'Good morning, sir,' and mean it. If you can get your people to say good morning *and* mean it, then you have achieved a great deal.

For centuries, naval captains of ships have habitually referred to their ships' companies as 'their people'. Being one of a body, a band of brothers or one of a great mass of people who are all equal, is something which is some-times foreign to our British stratified society, but if you are to get the best out of your people, then it is something you must cultivate, and the chief executive, the manager or the leader of any particular section must think of his companions as 'his people' and have responsibility for them.

*Banking on people*

Critical to this is discipline, though it may seem a strange word to introduce into a discussion about leadership. It is absolutely essential that we understand the need and the meaning of discipline if we are to exercise good leadership. Often the word discipline is identified with some kind of Prussian activity, but it comes from the word 'disciple' and is merely the acceptance of and insistence on a set of standards. There is no doubt that if one forgets the need for high standards, in cleanliness, in dress, in morality, in behaviour, then your chances of being a successful leader are diminished. Do as I say not as I do is really not good enough. If you wish to set yourself up as a leader or persuade yourself that you are a leader, then you have to be careful that the example you set is the one that you wish to be followed. (But, as you take the lead from the front, it's not a bad idea every now and again to look over your shoulder to make sure they're still behind you!).

If you have responsibility for an organisation and the people inside it, then you have to make contact with them. You have to be visible and be seen to be about your business. When you talk to people they must understand from your conversation that you are human as well as their leader and managing director or chief executive and that you are interested in them as individuals.

During my time in British Aerospace I did what I'd always done in a ship. I walked about it, and I walked about at odd times of the day and night. People knew that I was likely to appear in the most surprising places at the most surprising times. This meant that very rarely did I come across any of the disasters which can occur if you suddenly start to do things which you are not expected to do.

Goodwill and good human relations is like banking. You put money or goodwill into the account which you have with your people and you build it up so that when there are moments of extreme stress you can draw it down. You cannot, of course, overdraw too often or the goodwill will evaporate, but if your people have faith in you and your concern for them, then often you can overdraw the account and get away with it as long as you restore their fortunes as well as yours as soon as possible.

One of my most difficult experiences in exercising leadership was during my period in command of Ark Royal. We had installed new arrester gear that ended up looking like a bunch of tangled knitting after a few aircraft engagements on the flight deck. This meant that the engineers had to re-string the entire lot through hundreds of different pulleys, installed in the most inaccessible places. It was an agonising and unrewarding job and yet, as we were in the middle of a large NATO exercise and the centrepiece of the operation, the arrester wires had to be kept working. I remember going down to see the engineers at 4 o'clock in the morning. They had been slaving away almost continuously for fourteen days trying to keep this system working, while the powers that be tried to figure out why the damn thing was not working properly in the first place. I had been visiting them regularly during the course of this trouble but, on the last night, as they stood up when I walked in, I said: 'I have to tell you there is nothing more I can say to give you any encouragement, chaps. We're just going to have to see this thing through, and the burden is on your shoulders but we have no choice, we just have to get stuck in once again and sort this thing out'. And they did, because they knew that this was something on which the whole ship's reputation was going to depend. Sometimes you can offer people no hope but to get stuck in and do the job, and this is the most difficult aspect of leadership. To take over a company or a ship which is run down and not working very well and then lift it to high levels of enthusiasm and enterprise is not difficult; the trick is to keep it there. This is the real art of leadership.

Too often, as I walked around British Aerospace, I would sit and talk to people, sometimes my own age, sometimes older and when I had finished they would say: 'I know you're the chief executive because I've seen your picture but you're the first director of this company I've ever spoken to face-to-face, let alone the chief executive, and I have worked here for 40 years.' It almost made me weep to hear it. On one occasion I remember talking to a man who was fidgeting and looking nervously over his shoulder, and I challenged him to tell my why. 'What's the problem?' I asked. 'Are you worried about something?' And, after a pause, he said: 'Well, sir, we've been told to report everything you asked us and the replies we gave you'. 'Oh, really', I said, 'how interesting'. I never announced when I was going to visit a site to walk about but I always went to see the general manager at the end of my trip. On this occasion I said: 'If ever I discover again that you're asking your people to report what I say to them, let me tell you, you have something to worry about. If you are concerned about what your people will say to me then you won't be in your present position for very much longer.'

I am fortunate now to be associated with a company, TNT Express (UK), in which the qualities of leadership have been displayed in a most convincing way. This is nothing to do with me in this case, but it is a great pleasure to visit sites where people will tell me what the company should be doing in order to become more profitable and more successful. They understand that the world does not owe us a living and that the customer comes first. This is the real end product of business leadership - people who feel part of a successful team and who want to contribute to its future development.

Of course, the human side of business was once handled by personnel directors. I am opposed to personnel directors in the sense that they used to exist - as industrial relations managers - but I am not against them in the sense that they *should* exist now.

One of my first opportunities to express my view on this subject was when George Jefferson, then chairman and chief executive of the Dynamics Group of British Aerospace, invited his two managing directors of the two divisions and his personnel director, who was retiring, to interview a new candidate for the post of personnel director. We then were asked to sit like a bunch of sparrows in front of George's desk and asked in descending order of priority, starting with my colleagues, what we thought of the new candidate. My opposite number in the other division said: 'He is a super chap, just the man we are looking for'. The outgoing personnel director observed: 'He is a splendid chap and we should hire him'. He then, in an almost foregone conclusion, said: 'What about you, Ray?' And I said: 'He is one of the most impressive men I've had the pleasure of interviewing. But, we don't need him, we shouldn't hire him. You cannot sell your warts to passing gypsies George, your people are your concern and their conditions of service are your concern, and you cannot pass the buck. We, as managers, must be involved in personnel matters as much as we are involved in the production of our manufactured goods. There is no escape'. We didn't hire him.

## Working together

In the bad days of industrial relations after the war, it seems to me that the managers, the leaders of industry, were on a pig's back. The UK was the only intact industrial base in Europe and we could make things and sell them at our will. We didn't have to satisfy the customer, we just had to keep churning out the goods, and if industrial relations got in the way then we just bought them off and put up the prices. On the other side, there were men coming back from the Services who had experienced a totally different type of organisation - one in which there was not the kind of disinterest which had been manifested by the managers in industry - and they had been taught that, as a result of the war, things were going to change, and they were intent on changing them. This led to very strong and active trade unions which, instead of grasping the opportunity to manage change with the managers, reacted against them. Understandably so, in the circumstances. The management's response to this was to go out and hire professional personnel managers, so we had now created a situation in which two highly qualified adversaries were playing what I used to call the 'Whitehall tennis game'. The game of tennis was originally invented in Whitehall - the purpose of Whitehall tennis is to keep the ball in play, not to achieve a result. Industrial relations became a ping pong match between people who were trying to score points off each other, rather than facing the real difficulties the country was facing. It was, of course, primarily the fault of managers who didn't manage.

When I was a messenger boy at *The Times* newspaper, my father was Imperial Father of the Chapel. During this time the company secretary was a Mr Hoare, who hired everybody, fired everybody, and ran what in those days was called the Widows and Orphans Fund, the forerunner of our pension schemes. While these two men were in control, there was not one day's loss of work at *The Times*. When he retired at the end of the war, my father was disillusioned by what he found in men coming back and told me: 'They are intent upon fighting the battles we have already won'. Remember he had been a member of a trade union when you could be dismissed if it was discovered that you were a member. 'We have achieved most of the things, if not all of the things, we've set out to achieve in the trade union movement,' my father went on, 'What we should now do is work together with management to make us, collectively, more successful and profitable, but that is not what these new men coming back into our business seem to want to do. They seem to want to be adversarial'.

Fifteen or so years later, there was a massive industrial dispute at *The Times* newspaper which lasted for one year. At that time, I don't know how many managers there were but in the personnel department alone there were close to a hundred people. You don't solve industrial relations problems by the weight of numbers; you solve them by understanding your company's aspirations and making everybody part of the team that's going to achieve them, to their mutual benefit.

Management is about managing people. Leadership is about getting more out of people than any manager could possibly achieve by the mechanistic process alone. What is proper for personnel directors to do is to look into the circumstances surrounding employment in companies and to take charge of succession planning and training but not the management of people, that is the job of managers.

Another important aspect concerning the people side of leadership, is around appraisals and confidential reports. The Navy does not require that a confidential report need to be shown to the person who is being reported on, but the general contents of that report are to be made clear and, in particular, any criticism of that person's perform-ance which is in his or her's ability to correct should be drawn to their attention. In contrast, the Civil Service method is to show the report to the recipient and let them read it. I believe this leads to dishonesty. It leads to people not saying what they really think and going for a blander assessment than they would otherwise give. One of the difficulties in deciding who should be promoted is to sort out the wheat from the chaff. If 90 per cent of the people whom you are interviewing are going to be marked between 5.8 and 6.2, there isn't very much in the scale of one to ten to distinguish between them. I, there-fore, commend the naval policy of keeping one's own counsel. By being honest and signing that you have, at the end, informed the recipient of the adverse remarks you may have made, or criticisms which you have made which are within their power to correct.

There is a further safeguard that the Navy can apply. If an individual wishes to have his or her progress reviewed by a higher authority, or has a complaint against the system, then the confidential reports have to be produced. Clearly, if the individual has not been made aware of the criticisms that have been levelled, then that does not reflect very well on the reporting officer.

This may seem a minor issue, but leadership is about the simple things. It is about the humanities, it is about taking a personal interest in all your people by regarding them as part of a team of equals which you have been privileged to lead. To have them talk about 'our company', to have them understand the problems is an achievement which is music to my ears.

Nothing succeeds like success. People need to be touched; lead by example, but admit your faults openly. Give praise in equal measure, at least to admonition. Discipline is a key word that should not be misunderstood; efficient ships are not dirty ships - standards, standards, standards. Be open, give as much information as you can and make sure that promotion in your organisation is based on merit, and seen to be.

Watch your step - you can't have it both ways.

# RICHARD WELLS

## *On Leadership*

---

*Richard Wells* QPM *is Chief Constable of South Yorkshire Police.*

He joined the police service in 1962 after graduating from St Peter's College, Oxford.  His 28 years with the Metropolitan Police included service in both the West End and East End of London and at Notting Hill.  His experience embraces operational command, the leadership of Hendon Training School, and the interplay of community relations, media affairs and the 'front-line' delivery of services in a climate of reducing resources.

In 1990 he became Chief Constable of South Yorkshire Police.

In 1990, the long-serving and much respected chief constable of South Yorkshire Police retired. As the incoming chief constable I faced a unique challenge. The South Yorkshire Police had suffered the divisive ravages of the Miners' Dispute of 1984 and the calamity of the Hillsborough football disaster of 1989. Though morale is seldom a blanket phenomenon - affecting every part of an organisation in the same way at the same time - many heads were down.

Yet, since then South Yorkshire's 3,000 officers and some 1,500 civilian support staff have been awarded the Citizen's Charter Mark for excellence of service and make up the first police organisation in Europe to be admitted as members of the European Foundation for Quality Management. Such achievements are based on pride, dedication and excellence among officers and staff; and an alternative approach to police leadership based round the twin pillars of care and command.

## Care and command: an alternative approach to police leadership

**Taking over the reins: the importance of the first assessment, walking the new territory, striking an initial rapport and searching for facts and evidence for the need for change.**

Graffiti on a wall in London reads: 'Grey hair is hereditary; you get it from your children'. In the same spirit, it should be said that organisations shape their leaders.

Complex organisations take years to understand and the best a new arrival can do - at any level of authority - is take 'core-samples' of activity to get a broad grasp of the new command.  Talking to senior colleagues is an early necessity and it should be a structured discussion, taking them - at different speeds and on different occasions - through a planned but unobtrusive agenda of questions which help to map *their* perceptions.  Questions must be open-ended and must probe for evidence.  The object is to fathom what might be called others' 'meanings': deeper than 'opinion' and wider than 'view'; how the individual senses and responds to the organisation.

In between these 'mapping' sessions, fresh air is essential and a good starting point, particularly in a company which has far-flung outposts, is to head for the offices which are the butt of the local cultural humour - 'Have your passport ready if you are going as far as X'; 'She visited HQ from Y once but she missed the grass and trees'.  Questions here can be of a different intensity but are designed to test front-line perceptions of the 'meanings' held by those back at headquarters.  The perceptions can be dangerously gossip-riven and so anecdotes must be substantiated, as far as possible, by facts.

Nonetheless, such visits are invaluable for taking soundings from the existing culture.  The conventional police culture is essentially white, male and conservative.  The strong hierarchy is inclined to dominate by fear and produce all manner of 'insurance' behaviour - such as passing decision-making upwards to inappropriate ranks and the proliferation of paper. This sits uncomfortably with the remarkable courage and pragmatism of front-line officers when in the field. Such brave and decisive behaviour is valued when we senior officers sleep safely in our beds, but seems to be forgotten when day breaks; we trust our officers - salaried at around £20,000 - to risk their lives in confronting criminality, but typically won't trust them to order, without a supervisory officer's endorsement, a new pair of gloves at £3 to replace a damaged pair.

## Establishing trust

**Seizing the opportunity for remedial action: listening to front-line staff, using their experience as 'consumer panels', confronting bureaucracy and making incremental change.**

Confronting bureaucratic behaviour is best achieved by seizing opportunities as they arise. I visited the clothing and supplies stores in person to watch constables being served. In the presence of the stores supervisors, I asked the constables how they felt as 'customers' about the service with which the stores had provided them. The instance of the countersignature being required for a small item of kit was discovered in this way. It was reversed on the spot: new gloves were issued, without paperwork and new policy agreed immediately, formally confirmed later. Trust was established and expensive, time-consuming clerical work was eliminated.

Trust is critical to leadership. With trust, people grow. Without it, they may perform adequately but higher potential will wither. Many front-line staff - not least in the police service - feel that they are **not** trusted. If they feel mistrusted, they feel undervalued. Undervalued people under-produce and under-communicate. Leaders are then isolated from the talent and the feelings of those for whom they work, so creating a spiral of disaffection. The language of operational police officers, in casual discussion, often symbolised this spiral: 'Nobody listens to us'; 'The bosses don't really appreciate what our work is like'; 'We make a suggestion but nothing happens'.

Leaders who want to avoid this spiral can gain a great deal by performing occasional tours of duty with front-line service-deliverers. Attendance at a major football match in relentless rain soon showed the new chief the flaws in the duty anoraks issued. Budgets were adjusted to new priorities, officers were asked to choose the new anorak design and test it and then - the key point - it was issued quickly, starting with the front-line officers - senior officers taking a place back in the queue until those who needed the kit had it first.

Similarly, at the same event, two bites of the supplied snack were all that was needed to confirm that it was dull and unpalatable. A sergeant actually complained that his pack contained two 'growlers' instead of one (pork pies which even when eaten, failed to admit defeat)! Officers were asked to state their preferences - out went chocolate bars and fizzy drinks; in came wholemeal bread, salad fillings and fresh fruit. A bonus was that the new style packs cost significantly less per capita then the former contents. But the true gain was in the very simple, easily achieved, act of being there, listening and taking action. In a small but important way, officers felt more valued.

Such little, cumulative gains help the credibility of major change back at HQ - or, as it had become sceptically known in operational circles, 'The Wendy House' or 'The Dream Factory'. HQ staff were known as the 'ESSO' brigade - Every Saturday and Sunday Off. Each acerbic comment speaks volumes of mistrust and perceptions of distance between those in command and those performing day-to-day duties.

The Senior Command Team (SCT) - the top five chief officer ranks - set about working together. It was a process of mutual growth, often uncomfortable; there was no escape route, because the team inherits its new leader without choice, and the leader them. There are no severance packages, voluntary or involuntary redundancies. The members have to strike up a *modus vivendi*.

## Shaping the future

**Prescribing and sharing certainty: providing a vision of tomorrow, striking an informal 'contract' with the workforce and linking rhetoric to action in cultural change.**

One aspect which all organisations need, and which the formal leader has a responsibility for giving, is certainty. That certainty is best *shared*, bringing a greater sense of investment and ownership. But there is also a place for some *prescriptive* certainty - just enough to allow firm policy grip. To create a sense of certainty, the chief constable issued a statement of his vision for the forthcoming five years. It was a statement of intent, a vision of a better tomorrow.

The Senior Command Team then consulted widely, inside the organisation and - significantly - inside communities representing the general public, to get a grasp of what people in these groups saw as the South Yorkshire Police's purpose, its core values and the way it should be doing business. A mass of information was generated by this consultation from officers and staff at all levels. This was reduced by the SCT to a single (if lengthy) sheet of bullet points, tested by further consultation, refined, then finalised into, for the first time since 1839, a reference point for service standards, agreed by police and public alike.

Intermediate commanders and senior support staff were advised in advance that the document was to be sent to each member of the organisation, whatever rank, grade or role. They were to make action plans to cater for its reception, discussion and, above all, conversion into service activity.

The letter accompanying the document was effectively a contract between the chief constable and each of the 4,346 members of staff. Personally 'topped and tailed' in handwriting, the letter offered protection from retribution for mistakes, provided that they arose out of activity which was 'lawful, honest and reasonable'; in exchange, members were asked to try to see the general public as akin to a voting constituency, either for or against the South Yorkshire Police, and to try, each day whether on duty or off-duty, to win extra supporters.

Over the coming months, the rhetoric of the document - always in danger of cultural isolation - was reinforced by binding it into career progression. Promotion selection boards sought evidence of action which converted words to the reality of improved service; discipline tribunals referred to its breach in judgement and punishment. No-one was expected to learn it by heart; but people were expected first to know of it, then know its import and, finally, to be putting it into effect.

The SCT estimated that it would take at least five years for cultural change to gain critical mass. Despite surrounding Forces being busily engaged in restructuring, our commitment was to get cultural change underway first and, only when there was evidence of that success, to turn to reshaping the Force.

The change was to be effected in four main directions:

- ◆ from inward-looking self-protection to outward facing 'customer' focus

- ◆ from secretiveness and expedience to openness and honesty

- ◆ from fear-based tightness to trust-based flexibility

- ◆ from the upward drag/push of decision-making to devolution of reasonable risk.

## *Freedom and power*

**Setting people free: loosening up the organisation for greater creativity.**

The leader's responsibility in the organisation is to set people free to create and enable them to generate ideas for their own pursuit of excellence. The bonds which can inhibit innovation come in different shapes:

**Power plays** in which rank is allowed to outplay role. In a discussion, those of senior grade interrupt those junior to them or, in allocation of resources, allow themselves first choice; in queuing for food, they push to the front. So much can be achieved - as with the anoraks - by letting the front-line role have ascendancy; people's worth to the organisation can be quickly and effectively established by the simple gesture of preventing a senior executive from interrupting a junior contribution. 'Senior' is so often taken for 'superior' as if rank somehow magically acquired a monopoly of wisdom.

**Hierarchical modelling** encourages this win-lose stratification, and makes for enormous unfulfilled ambition, envy and unhappiness. An alternative is to see the organisation as a flat disc, with the chief executive at the centre and radiating grades out to a periphery, where service is delivered or products made. In this model each role is interdependent and human status and dignity derives from that shared responsibility as a team-member. The roles may be of different complexity and hence paid differently but the essence of the flat model is a greater equality of underlying human worth as a team-player. Value is partly reflected in financial reward, but significantly also in the effective, emotional reward of having one's contributory role actively appreciated, one's opinion sought and acted upon. In practice, senior personnel began to talk readily and easily of their staff as the people *they worked for.*

**Win-lose** is a product of an organisation which deals predominantly in parent-child relations instead of adult-adult dimensions. The style flows from the top - of the whole company or a group within it. Characterised by powerful individuals who seem always to need the last word, by sycophancy, cloning, hidden agenda, snouts and minders, inaudible bad-mouthing, lobbying and back-room deals, secret files and favourites, 'winning' is to gain a share of the power-base, however fragile, and clinging to it with white-knuckle ferocity. Whole nations can take over this mantle in the thrall of a dictator, where 'losing' can mean death.

**Turf protection**:  One of the sadder features of human-kind is what the author calls the 'personal sufficiency theory' - the market forces of individual adequacy.  Simply put, if an individual feels plentifully endowed with a commodity - food, money, time, love for example - there is a greater predisposition to share with a neighbour.  A key role for the leader is to help to free people from those individual market forces and to get them to think - and act - corporately; to turn individual skills into team talent.  Nothing is more damaging and divisive in an organisation than people putting their arm, metaphorically, around their own departmental or territorial plate for fear of a competitor taking their slice of overtime, personnel, attention, or praise.

If an organisation is to undergo and achieve true change, these organisational and personal restraints each needs to be loosened, untied or, if persistent, relentlessly severed.

Solutions lie, once again, in valuing people and explicitly rewarding unselfish behaviour, in encouraging (by inter-change between tasks, locations and roles) understanding of others' positions and in being scrupulously open and fair in the allocation of scarce resources.

*Setting the style*

**Conscious setting of a style of personal, then corporate, leadership.**

Starting with the chief - whether the chief executive or chief constable - there has to be a purposeful setting of the style of leadership. It need not be articulated but it must be quite explicit.

It needs to be marked by absolute honesty - not, it is to be hoped, about 'fingers in the till' but about the whole gamut of integrity. This would include, for example, the acknowledgement that a given policy is out of kilter with moral or legal precepts, however expedient; recognition of the other person's point in discussion as being more valid than one's own; the ready admission that one had misjudged a situation or a colleague; of one's weaknesses in a team as well as one's strengths.

Complementary to that intellectual integrity is emotional integrity: the ability of the leader to be able - at appropriate moments - to disclose more private aspects of feelings. Subordinates do not have the monopoly of fear, doubt, despair, uncertainty or anger and while they are entitled to look to the leader for courage, certainty, optimism and calm, they are not entitled to trap a boss on an emotional pedestal.

In a police context, at the stomach-churning accident or the carnage of a bomb blast, the operational leader has a responsibility for setting the standard and the style. In broad terms, this means getting on with the rescue work and returning to normality, whatever the personal feelings of nausea, anger and grief. Members of the public look to the uniformed services for support and are entitled to be reassured by their presence. But when the job is done and in the face of such extremity, there is no harm whatever in the chief standing alongside colleagues and either crying or being sick or both.

Honesty in that context will be quietly remembered by all who shared the moment. It is likely to encourage much better briefings and debriefings, where the integrity spills over into the practical sphere of plainly expressed anger or disappointment at things which went dangerously wrong, as well as warmly expressed delight at well planned success.

On that point, a phenomenon which seems to have escaped much of public office these days is that success belongs to the team and blame belongs to the leader. All too often, in immature, hierarchical structures, that cart is put before its horse: if there is the slightest hint of credit in the air, it is pounced upon by all in senior positions who wish to associate themselves, however remotely, with the glow of righteousness; if there is the slightest whiff of failure or blame in the wind, there is all too frequently the thunderous clatter of feet as the chiefs head for the apparent safety of the ramparts, from behind which they call for the names of the appropriately junior to stand up and take the stick. It is a transparently disgraceful way to behave, and worse, is seen by all for what it is.

While it is admittedly difficult always clearly to distinguish the two, there *is* a difference between standards and style. The leader is obliged to set standards and insist on their being maintained. These should be consulted upon and agreed and, thereafter, become non-negotiable. But, so far as possible, the *style* in which those standards are achieved can be much more a matter for the individual, since flair and talent have more in common with style than they do with observation of norms.

## Delegating responsibility

**Delegation, based on trust, to the most junior ranks possible for efficiency and effectiveness.**

Allowing individual style to shine through links closely with the role played by trust and delegation. The traditional police culture is strongly hierarchical; it has its roots in 19th century England, where there was a much stronger stratification in society by class; it drew its constables not just from the artisan stratum but also from - if the discipline records are anything to go by - soldiers of fortune, with a heartily wayward appetite for women and drink. Since the constables had such marked powers over those of the ordinary citizen and worked at a distance from their stations, they clearly needed tough supervision.

Our levels and standards of recruiting have changed dramatically and, because the constable is still, in law, granted high levels of personal discretion, it is appropriate to loosen the reins - of course within a framework of policy and explicit standards - to allow greater freedom.

In this way, the leadership in South Yorkshire has authorised its trained marksmen to arm themselves, at their own discretion, when confronted by armed danger, instead of waiting for higher, more remote authority. Since they will make the ultimate decision whether to shoot or not to shoot, and are accountable to the law for their decision, the choice to arm in the first instance is logically theirs too.

Deployment of other operational equipment - such as the 'Stinger' tyre-puncturing anti car-theft device, else-where authorised by senior ranks - is the responsibility of expert traffic constables in South Yorkshire. The policy decision manages a certain amount of risk, but has achieved time and cost savings with its directness and effectiveness. Even more important, the officers feel trusted and valued, and ironically, *more* accountable for their actions.

In transactional analysis terms, the traditional police culture is essentially 'parent/child'; the South Yorkshire model tries to move towards 'adult/adult'. There are occasions when 'parent/child' is just about appropriate - for instance, when going into a dangerous operational situation, with an explosive criminal mix of perhaps drink, drugs and firearms, there has to be clear, no-non-sense 'parental' leadership with assigned tasks met and fulfilled without hesitation. But at the preceding briefing and the subsequent de-briefing, it is the 'adult/adult' mode which will release the necessary criticism, controversy and credit. It is this mode which will stimulate ideas, often from the most junior and least experienced. Ideas and initiative are key resources to an organisation; leaders can unlock those resources or lock them out.

If people feel happier when they are able to provide ideas and when their talent is fully acknowledged and used, it would make an interesting piece of research to determine whether the corollary is true: that ideas from the workforce are more prolific when the workforce is happy than if people feel miserable and harassed. Deming's concept of 'joy in work' is critical to morale and arises directly from valuing people for their contribution to corporate effort. A direct but unobtrusive interest in their personal lives - tailored to each person's need for privacy - confers that value. In addition, so does the South Yorkshire insistence that staff take their full quota of leave, as they give so much during often long and demanding working days.

It is a leader's duty to reward through creating an agreeable working atmosphere, in which humour and fun are not simply permitted but sought after.

The leader - at all levels - needs strong personal support mechanisms. Inner strength and confidence will be essential and will grow at different paces and in different directions according to the rigours of the moment. Their development is proportionate to the pressure under which they are required to be exercised; when it hurts, it's probably what granny used to call 'growing-pains'!

But such pain can bring private self-doubt and loneliness. External support mechanisms are a valuable supplement to inner reserves and are an immeasurable blessing in the form of a stable family, a trusting and trusted work-team and a body of professional and extra-professional friends.

This support allows - or at least helps - leaders to fulfil a last and critical role: to absorb a proportion of the anxieties and aspirations of their staff and to serve as their champion in public debate and negotiation. For this, and for the sake of organisational morale, the leader has to project consistent optimism, confidence and strength of purpose. Such commodities do not come cost-free and will, over time, drain reserves of energy. Taking adequate rest and recuperation, whether from sleep or relaxation, are both a vital example by which to lead hard-pressed staff. These restoratives will conserve individual *and* corporate strength, optimism and confidence.

Confidence is catching. Chrysler workers created a one-off special car for their chairman. Delighted and touched by the thought, he nonetheless rejected the gift and asked them for a car straight off the production line; if *they* had made it, was the message, then it was good enough for him. There was a man who knew the worth of his staff and knew how to value them with a simple, symbolic gesture of his confidence in them.

A final quotation - attributed to Karkhùff - sets the seal on dynamic leadership which has at its heart both the strength to care and the will to command: 'Effective people do not grumble about the dark; they light candles'.

# SIR DAVID GILLMORE

*On Leadership*

---

*Sir David Gillmore GCMG headed the UK's Diplomatic Service from 1991 until 1994.*

He joined the civil service in 1970. Prior to that he worked in a variety of jobs. On leaving King's College, Cambridge, he worked for Reuters, before spending five years in Paris working for Polypapier. From 1965 until 1969 he was a teacher in London, during which time his novel, *A Way From Exile*, was published.

His civil service assignments began with two years at the Foreign and Commonwealth Office. He then held various positions throughout the world - including First Secretary at the British Embassy in Moscow and British High Commissioner in Malaysia. He returned to London to become Deputy Under-Secretary of State at the Foreign and Commonwealth Office in 1986 and, after a year at Harvard University and the WEU Institute in Paris, became Permanent Under-Secretary of State and Head of the Diplomatic Service in 1990.

Leadership requires mastery of a myriad of techniques. To this, leaders must bring a wide variety of natural attributes and some kind of inspirational ability. Techniques can be learned, but the other elements defy conventional training and, to a large extent, precise definition.

The great leaders have proved as unable to reach a clear definition or a precise formula of leadership as anyone else. It is reputed that Napoleon always asked how lucky his prospective marshals were. For him luck was as significant a part of leadership as decisiveness or bravery.

In my career, I have been extremely fortunate. Things have happened to me and I have done lots of different jobs - from teaching in a London school to leading the Diplomatic Service - but though I have been extremely fortunate, this does not necessarily make me feel as if I am a leader.

One reason for this is that leadership takes time. When you are younger, you may consider yourself successful and fortunate, but you probably don't think of yourself as a leader. Leadership implies a certain wisdom - and wisdom is not usually regarded as the preserve of youth. Also, leadership is often simply thrust upon you. It isn't necessarily calculated or clinical - you don't suddenly decide that you are ready to lead. You are given a job or find yourself in a role which demands leadership - whether you like it or not; and whether you possess leadership qualities, or not.

Leadership is not solely the domain of military leader, great politicians or of business people.  It is found in all aspects of our lives and all aspects of our working lives, no matter what our job or where we carry it out.

## The leader as teacher

In fact, like many people, I have found that leadership has impinged and played a part at virtually every stage of my life and career.  Teaching in the 1960s in a school in inner-city London, I was confronted with situations which required leadership.  Getting children to do their homework, maintaining discipline, exhorting parents to take an interest in the development of their children, are not issues one would normally associate with leadership.  But, while much depends on how and what you teach, there are elements of leadership in any form of teaching - and *vice versa*.

A leader has to teach to some extent.  Indeed, the current preoccupation in the business world is with the learning organisation - in which senior managers are coaches, mentors and teachers as opposed to narrowly-defined bosses.  Leadership is, therefore, not dictatorship but about sharing knowledge and expertise and enabling those who follow to achieve their full potential.

Great leaders inspire and make leadership appear available to all.  And, increasingly, leadership - or, at least, the skills it involves - is available.  While leadership may involve luck and is, to some extent, thrust upon you, it is possible to learn the techniques. There is now a large number of business schools and specialist institutions offering courses, and entire programmes, on the tools and techniques of leadership. The theory is available to all but, by learning it, you don't automatically become a leader.

The great leaders bring a wide range of natural attributes to the techniques they have acquired and the tasks they face. They are likely to possess intelligence, integrity, commitment and courage, among many other traits.

But these, by themselves, are not enough. As a leader, you also have to have something which inspires people. This is much more difficult to define. You are born with it - a sense, perhaps, of your own destiny. 'Before this time tomorrow I shall have gained a peerage, or West-minster Abbey,' said Nelson before the Battle of the Nile. For all the learning and the power of your own natural attributes you need this third element to succeed as a leader.

A neglected element in this pot-pourri of skills and characteristics is eccentricity. Leaders often possess a modicum of eccentricity. Their eccentricity is endearing rather than off-putting. Clearly, this is not something you can create, but it does mark out from the crowd leaders like Churchill and de Gaulle.

Perhaps it is eccentricity which allows leaders to take an alternative view - though in the jargon of leadership theorising it is called 'vision'. They are constantly able to appreciate and adopt a different, broader, more sensitive or more inspiring perspective on a particular situation or issue.

My father, who spent his career in the RAF, has always been a model for me. He is a man of the utmost integrity - an essential component of leadership - but he was never blinkered by the environment whether he was in the Flying Boat Squadron or at the RAF Staff College. Any environment, however stimulating in the short-term, is constraining. You have to be able to look over the walls, to look outside for new perspectives, examples and inspirations.

## Creating a band of brothers

One of the people who I believe embodied many of the characteristics of a truly great leader was Nelson. Perhaps he was not the greatest strategic thinker and, as a person, he had undoubted flaws. But, his achievements continue to amaze. He managed to keep the ships in his fleet at sea for unbelievably long periods - a year at a time, sometimes more. Yet, he sustained morale. There is a romantic notion of Nelson's captains and crews as a 'band of brothers', but the captains of his ships and their crews, must have been highly motivated, devoted and loyal to withstand and carry through such demands from their leader. To achieve this Nelson must have been an exceptional man with intense personal commitment.

Nelson proves that you can't lead at a distance. 'It is warm work; and this day may be the last to any of us at a moment. But mark you! I would not be elsewhere for thousands,' he said in the midst of the Battle of Copenhagen. You've got to be deeply involved in the organisation. Commitment is not one way; it has to go down and through the organisation. This requires presence - both physical and inspirational.

As leader of the Diplomatic Service I had continuously to contend with a major communications challenge. In terms of geographical location, the Diplomatic Service is a very widespread organisation with 220 individual missions round the world. Managing such a dispersed and diverse organisation is a problem. You need to get around to visit, yet the sheer size of the task is beyond any one individual. Though you can't be there in person, you can communicate personally and regularly. The head of a mission must know that you are aware of their existence and working on what is important to them. In such a dispersed organisation taking the opportunity actually to meet people is highly important. Personal communication is enormously time-consuming, but without it you become a faceless figure. If you are going to meet someone you are obliged to think about their problems and worries. You focus on them as people rather than distant names.

## Keeping the fires burning

I believe that being sensitive to and understanding people, while still demanding their utmost, is central to effective leadership. Selecting talented people and promoting the right people is crucial - the chairman of a large company once told me that the only really useful thing he could do was to choose a good successor! In the realms of leadership, in particular, the entire matter of selection is saddled with an apparently insoluble problem. The Foreign Office recruits highly qualified people and the competition is intense. But you can't test what the person will be like at the age of 45 when the real pressure starts. People occasionally burn themselves out. Sometimes, in their forties, the fire goes out.

Clearly, being at the top of any organisation brings with it colossal pressure. It is highly exhausting and so leaders need enormous stamina - Margaret Thatcher is one extraordinary example of the kind of stamina levels possessed by leaders.

Preparing early in your career for the pressures ahead is further complicated in public service by the fact that it is difficult to gauge where leadership begins and ends. There is a sense of frustration that you don't have the same degree of freedom as those in the private sector. You can't recruit or even fire people in the same way. Civil servants genuinely don't make policy so, no matter how senior your role, you are not the decision maker, though you are involved in the process of formulating policy recommendations and of implementing important and far-reaching decisions. As a result you have to be bureaucratic - you have to put ideas down on paper and record what you do.

Despite such limitations, public service is now a highly complex business. The diplomatic service is continually moving families around the world. Though its numbers are comparatively small - 6,400 UK-based staff - you are entrusting a man or woman with a great deal when they head a mission or embassy. They are a long way away and on their own - whether they are in Paraguay or Vietnam. Clearly, delegation is key - here, again, you can look to Nelson's example in picking his captains and backing them to the hilt.

Even though public service offers its own unique leadership challenges some of the basic principles remain. You need, for example, to be prepared to fight for your enterprise. You can set targets and objectives and go over achievements regularly so that lessons are learned - from the bottom of the Foreign Office to the highest echelon everyone has a clearly defined set of personal objectives.

Leadership is incredibly demanding and is perpetually creating different challenges, so that it is easy to be overtaken by the immediacy of the work in progress. Under pressure, exhausted and pressed for a decision, leaders need to make the time to draw breath. They must think about the job, look across the board, set objectives and move people towards them together.

# Sir Adrian Cadbury

*On Leadership*

---

Sir Adrian Cadbury joined the then British Cocoa and Chocolate Company in 1952. He was appointed to the board in 1958 and became chairman and managing director in 1965. He changed the company's name to Cadbury and, in 1969, the company merged with Schweppes - with Adrian Cadbury as deputy chairman and managing director responsible for implementing the merger. Appointed the company's chairman in 1974, he retired in 1989.

Since then Sir Adrian has been at the centre of the debate on corporate governance through chairing the Committee on the Financial Aspects of Corporate Governance. He has championed the role of non-executive directors and supports the separation of the roles of chairman and chief executive. As well as his work on corporate governance, Sir Adrian has also been a director of the Bank of England and chairman of PRO NED.

'*The history of mankind might be described by a cynic as a series of splendid expeditions towards the wrong goal, or no goal at all, led by men who had all the gifts of leadership - except a sense of direction,*' wrote Sir Richard Livingstone.

Livingstone's advice needs to be continually recalled by anyone in a leadership role. It is a sense of direction that we need to keep in mind when assessing leadership. The directional sense of leaders is more important than their powers of leadership and the two attributes do not necessarily go together. Livingstone's comment emphasises the profound difference between leading people successfully and leading them astray. Many have the desire to lead or the gift of leadership, but fewer, far fewer in the eyes of Sir Richard's cynic, combine them with vision and sound judgement. If you are told that a business is a going concern, it is as well to ascertain for yourself in which direction it is going.

Leadership, therefore, can be used for good, bad or uncertain ends. A distinguished Rabbi was once asked how to tell true from false prophets. He replied that there was no way and, if there were, there would be no human dilemma and life would not be worth living! With leaders at the more modest level there is, in my view, a useful measure which we can apply to the quality of leadership, to which I will return.

## Board leadership

My particular interest in leadership is in relation to being chairman of a company's board. The job of chairmen is to get the best out of their boards. It is a fundamental error to suppose that if you sit a group of competent, well-intentioned directors around a boardroom table, they will function as a board. Effective boards do not just happen; they are the result of hard work by their members and particularly by their chairmen. Chairmen are responsible for the work of their boards, for the issues they discuss, for ensuring that they have the information they need and for bringing matters to a decision when necessary.

In the language of management, boards are teams and chairmen are team leaders. Sir John Harvey-Jones has summed up the chairman's leadership role admirably: 'It is through the board that the company takes its drumbeat from the chairman.'

Chairmen are responsible for guiding their boards and for setting the pace for their companies, in the way that Sir John suggests. They also need to ensure that the beat of their drum is picked up throughout the enterprise. As for the nature of the drumbeat and the focus which boards should have, that again has been pinpointed by Sir John: 'The job of the board is all to do with creating momentum, movement, improvement and direction. If the board is not taking the company purposefully into the future who is? It is because of boards' failure to create tomorrow's companies out of today's that so many famous names in British industry continue to disappear.'

That telling indictment can be turned into a positive statement of purpose. It is the task of the board to create tomorrow's company out of today's. It is up to the chairman, as leader of the board, to ensure that it applies itself to that task, as opposed to involving itself in the fascinating minutiae of the management of the business. Board leadership, above all, is to do with setting the company's future course.

## Assessing the present

Planning for an uncertain future has to start from where you currently stand. From this point on I will be drawing, with its inevitable limitations, on my own experience as a chairman. When I unexpectedly became chairman of the Cadbury Group in 1965, I weighed up what seemed to me the pluses and minuses of the company's position.

On the credit side, we had important assets - strong brands which had stood the vital test of time (Dairy Milk chocolate dated from 1905, Milk Tray from 1915, Flake from 1920 and so on); competent well-trained management; technological skills in our core business (chocolate covered sardines, for example, were a potential new product; representing a technological triumph, if a gastronomic challenge); sound finances; and a strong sense of tradition and values.

On the other side of the coin the company was almost wholly dependent on a single raw material - cocoa - for its profits. It was, therefore, vulnerable to fluctuations in the price of cocoa, to pests and diseases affecting the crop and, most horrendous of all, to potentially misguided medical opinion as to the beneficial effects of eating chocolate.

Also on the debit side was the perception of wholesalers and supermarkets that the company was over-committed to independent corner shops and old-fashioned in its approach. Similarly, the City rated the company as sound but pedestrian. Internally, the company had a rigid overhead structure and a ponderous approach to making decisions.

## Planning for growth

The company could in Sir John's terminology have been categorised as an endangered species. We were failing to move fast enough into tomorrow. We needed to find ways to grow through geographical expansion, because growth prospects in the home market were limited, and through broadening the base of the business profitably. We had made a good start on the latter aim by developing a foods division, based on chocolate biscuits, cakes, Marvel and Smash. The last-named brands were built from scratch into market leaders, a considerable achievement in the competitive food trade; this level of innovation was not, however, being mirrored on the confectionery side of the business.

To speed up our rate of growth, we approached companies like Campbells in the United States to see if it would market our chocolate in America and allow us to market Campbell's food products in Europe. In this way, we could achieve wider markets for our chocolate brands and broaden our product range in Europe. These discussions had not reached any conclusion, when in 1969 Schweppes approached Cadbury and proposed a merger. Shares in Schweppes were widely held and its board was concerned about hostile bids. It had brand strength in soft drinks and had diversified into food in order to broaden the base of its business, as Cadbury had done.

The merger cancelled out many of the minuses I had identified. The combined company became less dependent on a single raw material, it had a worthwhile UK foods business at a stroke, plus two strong branded businesses capable of international expansion. The two firms together had the financial and managerial resources to invest in marketing, R&D and expansion into international markets. In addition, the merger speeded up the vital process of change at Cadbury, which had started but was making unacceptably slow progress in the face of rapidly increasing competition, on a global scale.

## Leading the merger

The merger set me a number of leadership tasks. The first was to persuade the major family shareholders that the proposal made sense, when their business was apparently capable of continuing successfully as it was. Then, as managing director of the combined business, I had to put together two companies which had been merged on a 50/50 basis. The same actions have to be taken as in a takeover, but there the authority of the company taking over is unquestioned. In a merger of equals, the commitment of both groups of staff needs to be retained, even though at times their main interest seemed to be in speculating about who had taken over whom, instead of getting on with the merger.

If it was hard to unify the business at home, it was even more difficult abroad. In Australia, both Cadbury and Schweppes had sizeable publicly-quoted companies. Neither shareholders, nor staff, could see any reason why a merger in far-off Britain should have the slightest effect on the way in which their businesses were structured and run.

In the process of putting the merger into effect, I learnt a number of leadership lessons. One was that a merger, or a major restructuring, provides readily understandable grounds for bringing about change. It is hard to effect change when things are apparently going well, as I had found. The merger provided a window of opportunity and such windows should be used to push through as much change as possible, while they remain open. I had the example of the merger in 1919 of Fry and Cadbury before me. Those businesses were not finally combined until 1965 and the longer a unit is left separate, the more entrenched it becomes in its separateness. Move fast, therefore, while you have the opportunity and consider finding a way of generating a shock to the system to bring about necessary change.

Another lesson was that moving boxes around on an organisation chart does not necessarily result in changed behaviour. People can continue to work as they did, even when they believe that they have changed. It is not just human cussedness, though that plays its part; it is genuinely hard to change an established pattern of working. The good sales representative finds it difficult to switch, on promotion, from selling to managing. To change behaviour you need to move people rather than boxes.

It helps in this kind of situation to decide from the start what to change and what not to, and to stick as far as possible with that decision. It provides a stable framework within which change can take place in a more orderly and, therefore, less threatening manner. There is nothing worse than confusion - and confusion stems from lack of leadership. The most difficult issue in a merger is deciding between people for posts, when you know one set well and the other hardly at all. Yet speed is essential in making such decisions to eliminate duplication and to unify the company.

## Changing course

The leadership task in a merger or period of rapid change is to provide direction and clarity of purpose to the enterprise. The leader has to instil a sense of company purpose at all levels throughout the organisation to override tribal loyalties. Such loyalties are an asset only if they can be harnessed. There is a motivational task as well; tomorrow's company not only has to be defined and understood down the line, it has to be seen as a goal worth working for.

With the merger, a significant step towards tomorrow's company had been taken. We had a broadly-based international business, strong brands, competent management and an emerging sense of identity. However, the competitive environment was changing and the company needed to take a new shape to succeed in the emerging world. In 1986, therefore, the company sold two of its four business streams and concentrated all its resources behind its international branded businesses - Cadbury and Schweppes. Confectionery and soft drinks were the two markets in which the company could compete globally. The outcome of that decision has been that the company remains in the world league in both types of business.

The sale of two substantial parts of the enterprise represented a major change of strategic direction for a company which was a grower of businesses, not a trader in them. It marked a decisive turning point and it is a test of leadership to sense when a change of direction of this kind is needed. Consistency and commitment are all-important in driving a plan through, but it is equally vital to know when to change course. Emerson wrote: 'A foolish consistency is the hobgoblin of little minds.' It is up to the leader to foresee when consistency turns into an unwillingness to read the signs of change.

The chairman of a board has to put change on the agenda at the right time and ensure that all the options, however uncomfortable - like selling cherished parts of a business - are thoroughly debated. The danger is that a favoured course of action emerges too soon and stifles serious examination of the alternatives. It is the chairman's job to see that the board is genuinely in a position to choose the best option from the company's point of view, however challenging to the prevailing orthodoxy.

## The role of the chairman

This brings me more specifically to the chairman's role. Chairing the board of a public company is a difficult and demanding task. The board will normally have both executive and non-executive, or outside, directors on it. It is up to the chairman to establish the equality of all board members, since all bear equal responsibilities. This involves encouraging executive directors to speak as directors, not as heads of divisions or functions, and minimising the disadvantage of outside directors in respect of their lack of detailed knowledge of the business. The balancing act for directors on a unitary board is to be sufficiently involved to know what is going on, while standing sufficiently far back to be able to exercise a critical, independent judgement. The chairman has to handle this tension between involvement and detachment, and that between board members speaking their individual minds and working as a team - between individuality and collegiality.

Chairmen have to ensure that issues are properly debated at the board, but they also have to determine when the debate must stop and decisions be taken.

### The chairman and the chief executive

There are two leadership roles in a company of any size, that of the chairman and that of the chief executive. They are distinct and different, although they may be held by one person. The chairman is responsible for the work of the board. The chief executive's task is to turn the board's decisions into action.

There are, in my view, compelling constitutional reasons for separating the two posts in the great majority of companies. If the same person is both chairman and chief executive, this represents a considerable concentration of power. It also makes it difficult for the board to carry out one of its key tasks - monitoring and, if necessary, replacing the chief executive.

There is a difference, too, in the time frames to which chairmen and chief executives are normally working. Chairmen continually have in mind the continuity of the company - what it might and should become in five to ten years time. Chief executives are only too well aware that failure to deliver this year's budget may leave their chairmen with no future to contemplate.

This point was admirably made by Antony Jay, best known now for the television series 'Yes Minister', but also a shrewd writer on management. He drew the distinction between the two roles in the following passage from *Corporation Man*: 'The difference is so profound that it is practically impossible to discharge both duties properly at the same time. The present and the future do not run in harness; their demands and emphases move at a different pace and sometimes pull in opposite directions, and it is rarely satisfactory if the conflict takes place in a single man's mind. If one man tries to do both jobs, one of them is likely to go by default.'

It is the focus on the company of tomorrow which is most likely to be at risk and on these grounds alone, chairmen should exercise their board leadership role unencumbered.

## Vision and values

The final point I would make in relation to the leadership role of chairmen is the part which they need to play in the communication of vision and values. Vision is central to ensuring that everyone in an organisation knows what the goals of the enterprise are and how their particular job contributes to them. In addition, a sense of vision is what inspires people to feel, both that the company's aims are their aims and that they are worthy of achievement. Companies are in business to achieve goals. The leader's task is to determine those goals, to communicate them and to win commitment to them.

This brings us to values. Here, the leader's role is to distil them and to instil them. I say distil, because the ability to create values from the top is limited, although they can be only too readily undermined from there, since the maintenance of values depends on example. Leadership involves articulating what the business stands for and acting as the guardian of those values.

Values are important, because they play an essential part in attracting people to a company and in retaining them. Every company has its own identity and if its reputation stands high with its customers, employees and all those with whom it does business, that reputation is a valuable asset which needs to be zealously guarded.

Values are important in another respect, as part of the framework which holds a company together as it grows. As companies extend geographically and as they devolve more responsibility from the centre to operating units, there needs to be some means of holding the entity together in the face of these forces for fragmentation. I believe that the glue which holds a company together is its beliefs and values, rather than its structures and systems.

There does, however, need to be congruence between aims, actions and values. Leaders are judged by what they do and this is measured against what they say. If the two are not in accord, there will be confusion down the line and cynicism about the leadership. Confusion and cynicism are the enemies of purpose.

## Leadership qualities

In determining the predominant qualities which mark out the effective leader my choice would be: sense of direction, competence, values and conviction.

I have already emphasised the importance of leaders knowing precisely where they are heading. Sense of direction encompasses a feel for strategy, for that is needed in the choice of goals. It includes the ability to look beyond the immediate issues and to analyse the future options objectively. The lead - the step ahead - which is the badge of the leader is derived from foresight. Leaders anticipate turning points and foresee the need to change direction before others do. They set a firm course, but sense when a change of course is called for. Leaders who lack the gift of foresight stick blindly to their chosen path, in defiance of changing circumstances. As Conrad wrote: 'Any fool can carry on, but only the wise man knows how to shorten sail.' He might have added 'when' to 'how'.

Competence, or perhaps more accurately perceived competence, is an essential attribute for acceptance as a leader. It forms the basis of trust. We put our confidence in those whom we believe have the experience, skill and judgement to guide us. No-one would follow a leader unless they believed them to be competent to plan the route, to have foreseen possible pitfalls and to cope with the unexpected. In an increasingly professional world, competence and the capacity for judgement, which is grounded in competence, are the foundations of leadership.

Respect for a leader's values maintains our allegiance as a follower. If our trust in a leader is based initially on their competence, it is retained by regard to their integrity and for what they stand for. Coercion provides leadership of a kind, but it only lasts as long as the force backing it is effective. We escape from coercive leadership as soon as we may, because we recognise that we are being used for the leader's benefit. We remain voluntarily under leaders with whose values we identify. We need leaders to set standards which we admire and to which we willingly adhere.

I have added conviction, because there is a dimension beyond sense of direction, competence and values. Those qualities have to be brought to life and it is the conviction of leaders which convinces us that we should put our trust in them. Sense of purpose needs to be buttressed by determination. If leaders are to carry conviction, they have to be able to state their goals clearly and persuasively, and to win commitment for them. More fundamentally, they have to frame those goals in conjunction with those for whom they are responsible. Leaders need to listen -

an underrated art - and to understand the aims and motivation of those they are leading. True leadership is not about issuing commands from on high, but giving precision and form to the aspirations of those being led.

Separating good leadership from poor leadership emerges clearly over time. True leaders encourage their followers to develop their talents and to grow in stature. They build their successors, so that, in time, their leadership will no longer be needed. False leaders take away from their followers the ability to decide for themselves; they hold them in thrall and diminish them as people. The tests in essence are simple ones, good leaders grow people, bad leaders stunt them; good leaders serve their followers, bad leaders enslave them.

# JOHN ARKELL

*On Leadership*

---

After serving in the Second World War, John Arkell CBE TD CIMgt was appointed personnel manager of J Lyons & Co in 1945. In 1949 he began a long association with the BBC when he became controller of staff administration. He later joined the BBC's Board of Management and was director of administration from 1960 until 1970.

Upon leaving the BBC, he was on the board of a number of companies including Boots and the Coates Group, and was chairman of the Air Transport and Travel Industry Training Board. He was a lay member of the National Industrial Relations Court throughout its existence. He was also a visiting fellow at Henley Management College and worked as a consultant for various organisations. John Arkell has been an influential member of the Council for the Protection of Rural England since 1946 and chaired the committee which produced the Arkell Report in 1983 for the National Trust.

## What is general management?

### Definition

General Management is not a strict observance of rules and regulations, techniques, procedures and the like - though they can be useful and sometimes essential servants. It is much more than dealing with computerisation, cash flow, cost effectiveness or human resources, to name a few aspects of it. It has to do with the whole picture, the whole ship, to see that she keeps afloat. It concerns grasp of situations with constant watching to see that nothing gets out of hand. But it is even more positive than this. The ship must not just stay afloat, she has to sail forwards at a speed which over a planned period will give optimum returns and this involves inter alia strategic planning, economic production, and marketing.

There is no 'one thing' about management that can be singled out as the key, such as could be said about the professions of law and medicine. There is no talisman. It is more diffuse. This is partly its attraction and the source of its excitement. I am not of course talking about the various specialisms in Management such as accountancy, and engineering which have to be learned, but the balancing and control of these disciplines towards a given end. There have been many definitions of Management. Some take leadership as their cornerstone. A succinct one is that of Sir Ewart Smith "The organisation and control through leadership of human activity directed to specific ends". This can be applied to anything - coal, chemicals, catering, the Civil Service, or broadcasting. But a neat skeleton phrase cannot come near to describing the whole spectrum, the diversity, the risk element, or the imaginative concepts that are involved.

I made one attempt to put clothes on the skeleton when presenting the British Institute of Management Certificate of Merit for a Management Film competition: I said "These films comprehend a wealth of pragmatic and logistic information especially about that aspect of management which can in fact be taught and trained. They also hint at the more elusive, some of them inherited, qualities of a really outstanding manager - qualities that are born in many people but which need training and exposure to see the light of day. What *is* Management in this sense? What *is* the curious mixture of qualities which combined will produce such success, and will sometimes lead to an entrepreneurial flair? *I* can't describe it. But it is an amalgam, isn't it, of seemingly contradictory attributes - of the exploitation of short term opportunities with long term wisdom, of thrust with humility, of the capacity to ensure that a whole range of action is carried out and total accountability for it with devolution and delegation of authority, of dogged determination and persistence (never giving up especially in a matter of great principle) with the knowledge of when to compromise, the quality of power with people rather than over people, the combination of vision and grasp...."

135

By a pure coincidence Sir Terence Beckett, one-time Director General of the CBI, spoke on the same theme independently in a speech sometime ago and in a subsequent letter to me wrote, "It is extraordinary how both you and I see some of these qualities of management in terms of contrasts and the need, in fact, to combine some of these apparently opposed characteristics if a manager is to be successful". Sir Terence quoted a description of the qualities needed of a General attributed to Socrates: "He must have imagination to originate plans, practical sense and energy to carry them out. He must be observant, untiring, shrewd." Socrates adds these antitheses, "He must be kindly and cruel; simple and crafty; a watchman and a robber; lavish and miserly, generous and stingy; rash and conservative". As General Wavell once commented, Socrates put all of these qualities before the knowledge of tactics and even strategy. (Incidentally Wavell used to read Homer in the original Greek every day of his life, not unlike Alexander the Great who apparently carried the Iliad with him on his campaigns.)

It is not just that these 'opposites' denote the need for flexibility, though that can be important. It is more the recognition that there is no static body of knowledge that will give the top manager the infallible solution to a problem. The generalist not only has to call upon the various specialisms and techniques that suit the circumstances, but he or she also has to invoke personal qualities appropriate for achieving a particular objective from the many facets of his character which may seem at times paradoxical. Someone who is always single minded and unable to rationalise and compromise will fail as a top manager, just as someone will who cannot recognise the time to be strong minded and persistent.

This does not mean that the successful manager must by nature be insincere or lack integrity of character. The opposite of course is true. He/she must never confuse the need for different approaches and attitudes of mind with any departure from honesty. I remember at one of the BBC Senior Management Training Conferences a producer putting a leading question to the speaker, the comedienne Joyce Grenfell, to the effect that flexibility and change were surely the essential keynote for progress. Her reply which was significant to what I am trying to stress here - was that you have to distinguish between the naturally ephemeral things where it is necessary to be responsive to innovation and fashion, and the timeless truths which you change only at your peril.

## Trust

If I am labouring this point, it is because the integrity of the manager is of the essence. In a large industrial organisation composed of a workforce whose contribution is proportionate to the 'climate' and leadership they encounter there, high ethical standards are paramount. I once chaired a working party of top executives and Union leaders in the Air Transport and Travel Industry to examine weaknesses in industrial relations with a view to reducing the number of strikes. Of the many conclusions reached, one simple message ran through the discussions as a recurrent theme that if management tells the staff it is going to do something, it must do it. It must stick to its word. Half the trouble particularly in the Unions' view was this, and the lack of trust which followed from it. Admittedly this was at the time when Unions were very powerful and some very unreliable, but the principle holds. Unlike the picture that is still fairly prevalent at our Universities of a low standard of ethics in industry and commerce, in fact it would be difficult to think of any operation that clamours for a higher standard in these respects than a large industrial organisation.

Perhaps an anecdote at this stage may not come amiss to illustrate the vital importance of human relations and of fairness, in the minds of staff whether in relative rates of pay, promotion opportunities, or general working conditions. Not long after I was appointed Personnel Manager of J. Lyons and Co., the then most profitable and largest catering firm in the world, I was summoned to a Board meeting, to meet in the event a baptism of fire. The Board meetings of Lyons were famous in those days for the way in which a problem was thrashed out at an interminable length so that the solution almost rose like a phoenix from the ashes of exhaustion. I was somewhat apprehensive as I walked along the fourth floor of Cadby Hall and heard the shouting and banging that emanated from the Board Room which sounded to me like the Last Trump.

"I want you to hear what our new Personnel Manager thinks is fair to staff", Sir Harry Salmon the chairman said as with difficulty he silenced the Board members when I entered.  The room had a vast table in the shape of a coffin seating many Salmons and Glucksteins - with a few Josephs inter-mixed.  He then sketched out a complex problem that had arisen in the three Lyons Corner Houses, and asked me what I thought was fair to staff.  I could not think what to say, and I foolishly murmured that I would rather like notice of the question.  This produced a minor uproar, with one director close to me muttering "That's no good.  You've got to think on your feet here".  So I made a stab at it and produced a solution off the cuff, which almost lifted the roof in its reception by the Board.  Apparently it would have cost £100,000.

At this point Harry Salmon, being most courteous to me, said "Well, gentlemen, we really must take some notice of what our new Personnel Manager thinks...", but his words were drowned in the previously sotto voce comments around the table suddenly becoming audible with statements like "We didn't want a new Personnel Manager.  Who said we wanted a new Personnel Manager?"

Again Harry Salmon amid the uproar came to my rescue, saying "Well, you've got one now and you must take into account what Mr. Arkell thinks is fair to staff", to which amidst the clamour that this provoked one director, the largest of the bunch - an enormous man - bringing a huge

fist down on to the table with such force that all the ash
trays bounced into the air, replied exactly this "Oh Uncle
Harry, how can you say that? We never used to be fair
to staff, why should we start being fair to staff now?"
There was an enormous roar of laughter which must have
drifted down all the corridors and out into the bakery
below. Tension was eased. The ice was broken. The
laughter was in reality a measure of the care they took
about staff, because the directors knew that their highly
successful business was largely due to this very anxiety
itself to be fair to their employees for which they had a
deservedly high reputation. The Salmons and Glucksteins
were dedicated people who had selected a first class staff,
including after all Margaret Thatcher in their laboratories.
There was a need for a more up to date concept of
personnel management, but in many ways the Company
had led the way. Their personal caring for their staff was
remarkable, and I remember one informal Board meeting
being broken up because one of the directors had received
a note that a foreman in his division had just been told
that his wife was seriously ill. The director, who interestingly was the same man who made the solecism about
never being fair to staff described above, immediately
hurried out to see him. I do not believe the family would
feel I was in any way betraying a confidence in describing
the above atmosphere at this particular board meeting,
because it is a compliment to their dedication, tremendous
enthusiasm, and caring leadership. It also illustrates the
diverse personal, sometimes contradictory qualities that

need to be summoned-up by great leaders (and they were great leaders) described under the definition above.

## Management training

Leadership is a vital component not just at the top of an organisation but at all management and supervisory levels. Some of the trained leaders at the lower and middle levels will become the top management of the future. So the training is important. When I was Director of Administration in the BBC I was able to initiate training in management at virtually all levels, and particularly for Controllers and Heads of Department. For the latter, I established residential conferences mainly at Uplands in Buckinghamshire. For the first one Oliver Whitley, Controller Staff Training and Appointments, and I went to enormous pains to make it a success. We made careful choices for the outside speakers, for example Lord Robens then Chairman of the Coal Board and many others, arranged practical sessions, and went into meticulous detail about the administration so that there would be an air of competence and efficiency from the start. We were bent on ensuring that the first conference would be so successful that other senior BBC staff would want to attend in future. The input was a mixture of talks from outside and inside the BBC. About 20 men and women attended each course, divided into syndicates.

We certainly succeeded, largely due to the creativity of Oliver Whitley, and gradually from then on senior staff contrived hard to get accepted for successive courses at Uplands. To attend became almost a symbol of success. These Management Training Conferences were composed of senior staff from every part of the BBC - Television, Radio, External Services, Engineering, the Regions, News and Current Affairs, Administration. A by-product therefore was the fostering of a sense of unity throughout the BBC. But the main objective was to improve and develop the art and science of management and leadership.

These conferences continued for many years and became an outstanding success and feature of BBC life, improving inter alia the fields for promotion to the topmost appointments in the BBC. Although the ability to manage and lead is partly inherent, training is essential to bring it out, create and develop it.

## Devolution

Linked to Management Training is the need in a Company of any size for devolution. Apart from the freedom it gives to the top Manager to plan, think ahead and perform a strategic role, it facilitates the middle and junior managers to learn leadership through experience. Much can be achieved by a judicious mixture of structural devolution (the responsibilities being written into the prescription of the duties of the post) and the art of delegation (by which discretion is used as to how much more or less than prescribed is in fact delegated depending partly on the faith or otherwise in the ability of the staff concerned). The optimum level for decisions to be taken is often nearer their actuality and lower down the hierarchy than is realised. In this connection, in formulating the structure of a Company provision should where possible be made for a ladder of promotion up which managers can benefit from attaining gradually higher responsibilities. In all this, people are more important than structure. Good leaders can operate a bad structure. Bad leaders cannot work a good one. This is one reason why there is often need for flexibility and change.

## Enthusiasm and talking to staff

An additional important feature of enterprising management and leadership is enthusiasm. I noticed this particularly in the States during my periodic researches there. Enthusiasm is sometimes lacking within British organisations, though less so now than it was. An enthusiastic leader will attract a great following, and if his or her disposition contains an element of humour as well, so much the better. Also important is the ability to speak convincingly to staff collectively. This skill can partly be acquired through training. It is used in industry too seldom and can be invaluable in creating motivation as well as an aid to solving problems and collecting the wisdom of a group.

## Two examples of leadership

Industry has produced great leaders, some of them in the flowering period of the latter part of the last century when many new large companies were born. In some cases their influence still permeates the companies a hundred years later. One example is Jesse Boot who founded an industrial empire which still retains some of the benevolent characteristics stemming from a deeply religious and philanthropic man. The Boots Co. of today possesses the highest standards of service and integrity as well as being one of our most efficient and prosperous companies.

The same applies in other fields. For example Lord Reith, first Director General of the BBC, in spite of his personal eccentricities and weaknesses of for instance vanity and impatience as revealed by Ian McIntyre in his excellent biography, was a superb leader who strongly defended the independence of the BBC from both Government and commercial pressures, and made public service broadcasting a shining example to the world. His influence also prevailed in the BBC long after he left it in 1938, and had its effect in broadcasting policy throughout the world. Although I never served under him in the BBC, I knew him well: he possessed outstanding leadership qualities some of which were vision, tremendous industry, clarity of thought and a first class brain, tenacity, a great presence, determination and, when he wished to exert it, charm and a sense of humour.

In short, the influence and impact of really great leaders makes an imprint upon the future and lasts for many generations.

## Conclusion

I would like to conclude by emphasising and elaborating on a few points. The manager needs a whole range of qualities of character in his armoury if he or she is to utilise resources both human and material successfully towards specific objectives on any scale. No computer can ever be fashioned to supplant the quality of mind that is needed for this kind of leadership, involving many characteristics that at first sight seem contradictory. Management training to identify and improve leadership qualities is vital, especially in a virile and developing organisation.

Then it is *people* who determine the success of any enterprise. You need of course the machinery of production, the technical know-how, marketing knowledge, and the vital finance to float the ship. But it is people who will make her go forwards at the right speed. This means leadership at all levels of management providing a policy of general fairness to staff and a quality of direction which takes account of the wisdom and aspirations of others in the organisation. This leadership can be tough, thrustful, firm, enthusiastic, sensitive, magnetic, often self-effacing. There are many ways of leading peculiar to the individual. But it must be competent, caring and robust. In spite of the width and diversity and the opposites in its make-up, it must have a great moral quality about it really to succeed. If charismatic is too religious a word to use, it must have the grace to lift it above pettiness to the big issues of strategy, sometimes of life and death which exist in any large organisation.

# PROFESSOR
# SIR FREDERICK
# CRAWFORD

*On Leadership in Universities*

---

*Professor Sir Frederick Crawford has been vice-chancellor of Aston University since 1980. He retires from this position in 1996.*

Professor Sir Frederick Crawford has served as Vice-chairman of the Committee of Vice-chancellors and Principals (1993-95) and is currently its second longest serving member. He is director of the Higher Education Quality Council. Immediately prior to his Aston appointment, he spent twenty years in California at one of the USA's top private universities, Stanford, where his scientific speciality was plasma physics.

He is a non-executive director of Legal & General Group plc, Bowater plc and PowerGen plc. In 1992 the Institute honoured him with a Special Award for University Management. He was knighted in the 1986 New Year Honours.

Universities exist primarily to supply a service and a product, respectively the education of their students, and the disseminated output of their scholarship and research. Their working material is knowledge, and their activities generally fall within the following categories, though in widely-differing proportions in individual universities:

- ◆ **Generation** - 'research' - which involves the discovery of new knowledge; for example, by laboratory experiment or field-work. Areas and directions of research are inevitably constrained by the availability of funding. According to the source, projects may vary from curiosity-driven basic research, only lightly steered by the sponsor, through generic research, supported because it is likely to benefit a particular field of application, such as the pharmaceutical industry, to a tightly-specified contract for applied work, such as for a single company.

- ◆ **Marshalling** - 'scholarship' - which involves the purposeful arrangement of existing knowledge. At one extreme of the spectrum, new patterns may be discovered that are so significant as to be best categorised as research results; at the other, the intention may simply be to present knowledge to other scholars and to students in a form which can be more readily understood and assimilated.

- ◆ **Transmission** - 'teaching' - this encompasses far more than simply lecturing to classes, and should be regarded more generally as management of the student learning process. Students may be undergraduates acquiring a professional discipline and learning to learn, or postgraduates broadening and deepening their knowledge, or participants in continuing education and training, typically enriching their knowledge selectively through short, non-degree, post-experience courses.

◆ **Application** - including the utilisation of staff expertise in fee-earning activities such as clinical, consulting and testing services, and through memberships of government committees, advisory groups, and professional organisations at local, national and international levels. When these activities are not fully reimbursed, the shortfall can be regarded as a business investment to the extent that it enhances the university's reputation and facilitates subsequent income generation.

149

From the relatively firm ground of what universities do, we shall now step into the quicksands of how they do it, and how they may be compared with companies. Clearly, universities and companies vary widely among themselves, and by defining and comparing distinguishing features I risk provoking comprehensively my academic, industrial and commercial colleagues. I believe, however, that trends extending over the last decade are promoting a convergence in operation and management which has powerful implications for the leadership of both universities and companies.

## How a university is like a company

In recent years, the Trading Company Model (TCM) of a university shown in Figure 1 has evolved rapidly as a result of government legislation. Although Higher Education (HE) is still considered to be primarily the financial responsibility of the State, the manner in which funding flows to individual universities has been made increasingly transparent, and subject to formalised research and teaching assessment processes. Previously, universities received block grants whose composition was not made explicit. It is now feasible to construct a TCM similar to that of Figure 1 for each department, indicating whether or not it is effectively contributing to, or receiving funds from, other departments.

Over the last decade, the percentage of eighteen-year-olds entering HE in the UK has nearly doubled. Over the last four years, the number of institutions in membership of the CVCP (referred to throughout as 'universities', though not necessarily so titled) has increased roughly from 60 to 100. Why? It is now widely understood that, in an increasingly knowledge-intensive world, national competitiveness and prosperity, and individual access to jobs, depend critically on the education and training of the workforce. Substantially increased participation rates in HE have resulted. At the same time, competition among universities for the funds available for teaching and research has greatly intensified and individual university departments are now stimulated to scrutinise sharply how the funding that they generate is distributed via their local TCM.

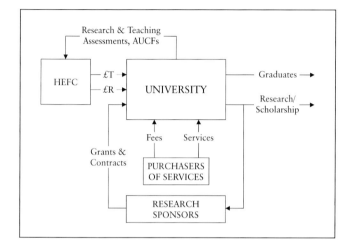

*Figure 1: The Trading Company Model*

Government support for teaching (£T) is channelled primarily through Higher Education Funding Councils (HEFCs) for England, Wales and Scotland, and through the Northern Ireland Office. The HEFCs regulate home student numbers and per capita funding, imposing annual efficiency gains related to any excess of local per capita funding in a given subject area over the corresponding national Average Unit of Council Funding (AUCF). In this respect, in relation to their teaching costs, universities are currently constrained to operate like regulated utilities on an annual funding formula of approximately RPI minus four per cent.

The HEFCs also provide a 'dual support' base (£R) to cover salaries for research-active academic staff and basic facilities for their work. Its level is dependent on ratings established by periodic Research Assessment Exercises (RAEs). Six Research Councils distribute further research funding competitively via grants and contracts which include a modest overhead element. In recent years, a substantial fraction of the dual support base has been transferred from the HEFCs to the Research Councils, to contribute to the overhead element. Other Government departments, industry and commerce, and the EU, also sponsor substantial volumes of university research with widely-varying overhead levels. Since the introduction of RAE-dependent HEFC research funding in 1986, competition among universities for research grants and contracts, and managerial efforts to achieve favourable ratings, have greatly intensified.

In company language, this is the competitive marketplace in which universities trade their teaching and research wares, and leadership is to be exercised. How that is done is influenced by the opportunities offered, and the constraints imposed by local managerial structures. Aston's managerial structure is not atypical, and is shown in Figure 2 (page 154). It is analogous in many respects to that of a company. The Council (= Board of Directors) is legally responsible for the university, and therefore for its financial solvency and such other long-term, university-wide issues as estates and buildings, and personnel policies. It contains lay members (= non-executive directors) who bring experience from the outside world, one of whom, the pro-chancellor, is chairman. The vice-chancellor (= chief executive) is an *ex officio* member responsible for maintaining and promoting the efficiency and good order of the university, usually with the aid of two or more pro-vice-chancellors who are also *ex officio* Council members. The lay office of chancellor (= honorary president) is primarily ceremonial; the holder does not directly influence the corporate governance of the university (ironically, Aston's chancellor is Sir Adrian Cadbury).

Though Council has ultimate responsibility for academic developments, it does not occupy itself directly with them. They are the province of the Senate, which reports to it. It is chaired by the vice-chancellor and does not contain lay members. Academic teaching and research programmes (= service and product lines) are developed primarily in departments on a disciplinary basis, with an overlay of interdisciplinary teaching and research. Departments with close or overlapping interests are grouped into faculties (= divisions), which are served by Faculty Boards chaired by deans (= divisional directors) who are *ex officio* Council members.

153

The membership of Council is completed by academic staff elected by the Senate and other constituencies (= worker representatives), together with a variety of non-voting members, some *ex officio* and others elected by support staff (= worker representatives) and students (= customer representatives). In this context, support staff may be non-academic staff from academic departments, or from substantial free-standing support services, such as finance, library, information systems, or external relations. Similarly, Senate membership contains a mixture of *ex officio*, and elected representatives, supplemented by a variety of non-voting members, some *ex officio* and others elected, for example, by the student body (= customer representatives).

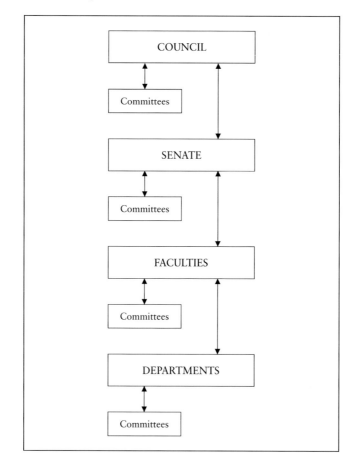

*Figure 2: Managerial Structure*

So far, the analogy has been pursued between a university and a company with several operating divisions, offering diverse service and product lines. As with companies, an important element of policy-making should be the promotion of synergy, so that the university is more than the simple sum of its parts and operates optimally, even if this conflicts with attempts in some of its academic departments and support services to achieve local optimality.

Such conflicts are typically variants of 'the prisoner's dilemma', the archetypal game in which a selfish player does best if the other acts unselfishly (win/lose), whereas both can at least do well if they cooperate (win/win) but will do badly if they both act selfishly (lose/lose). Leadership at the top in universities is largely about detecting and encouraging departmental developments that are potentially win/win and promote synergy, and discouraging those that are potentially win/lose and lose/lose activities, conducive to conflict, fragmentation and inefficient use of resources.

How can that be done systematically? One suggestion drawn from modern management thought is that organisation-wide optimality may be pursued more effectively via a process, rather than a function, approach. The process approach, exemplified by Total Quality Management (TQM), aims to soften the rigidity of functional and departmental boundaries by demonstrating the intrinsically cross-functional and inter-departmental nature of key processes, for example, the reinstatement of students.

The importance of internal customer/ client relation-ships, and the futility of strengthening some links in the process chain disproportionately while others are weak, are emphasised.

The TQM approach has been advanced implicitly in universities over the last few years by teaching assess-ments, in which Quality Audit visits are arranged by an independent Higher Education Quality Council to deter-mine whether or not there are university-wide mechanisms in place that should ensure that teaching quality is promoted effectively. These visits are complemented by subject-specific Quality Assessments arranged by the HEFCs to establish whether or not quality is actually being delivered. In contrast, the periodic Research Assessment Exercises conducted by the HEFCs effectively benchmark perform-ance against national and international research standards, and do not examine the detailed processes by which these standards are achieved. They do, however, by virtue of the direct link between ratings and HEFC dual support funding, strongly encourage the purposeful management of research activities in universities.

Although teaching assessments are only at an early stage, the published Audit and Assessment reports may be expected to influence prospective students in their choices among the universities, and it is reasonable to anticipate attempts by the HEFCs to link student numbers and per capita funding to teaching quality ratings. Cur-rent disagreements between the CVCP and the HEFCs centre on whether or not it is feasible to assign such ratings and, if so, by whom they should be determined.

So far, I am aware of little explicit use of TQM in UK universities. The remarkable efficiency gains made in recent years derive mainly from fat-trimming, incremental and decremental budgetary adjustments in academic departments and support services, and unsustainable temporary skimping in areas such as equipment replacement and building maintenance. Under financial pressures, powerful stresses are building up. Like companies, it is to be expected that universities will evolve towards purposeful use of TQM philosophy, tools and techniques, and service level agreements between departments, as soon as academics realise that they have been speaking prose for forty years: stripped of its jargon, TQM is simply a managerial application of the scientific method.

A widely discussed feature of modern management is that of workforce empowerment. Its advocates contend that the exercise of judgement in carrying out processes, and responsibility for process improvement, should be delegated to the lowest level at which the necessary expertise is located, and that such empowerment encourages initiative, motivates the workforce and promotes optimal operation. It may be contrasted with Taylorism, in which processes are designed at a higher level in such elemental form as to minimise worker judgement and initiative.

Empowerment will only lead to optimal operation of an organisation if local objectives are consistent with organisation-wide objectives. How can this consistency be encouraged? A co-operative, shoal-of-fish model is desirable, in which each worker is subject to minimal constraints but recognises the security and sustenance benefits of swimming in the general direction of the rest. This objective, common to both universities and companies, has led in recent years to increasing emphasis on organisational mission and vision statements which can be communicated and understood in appropriate detail throughout the workforce.

It is hoped that such statements will promote informed co-operation among those who have been empowered, and stimulate them to make a multitude of incremental process improvements ('kaizen', in TQM parlance). Much recent management literature has suggested, however, that radical process improvement is more likely to result if creative professional staff are charged with looking afresh at processes, and exploring innovative ways of re-engineering them, eg by the introduction of information technology.

Both universities and companies would probably agree on how they go about making incremental and more radical process improvements: the most senior leaders and managers of the organisation proceed by iterative cycles of the following basic steps:

- ◆ Define the organisation's vision and mission,

- ◆ Communicate them to the workforce

- Define objectives and goals

- Develop plans to achieve them

- Distribute required expertise and authority to act

- Monitor performance

- Modify preceding steps to improve performance.

*How a university is not like a company*

Despite the similarities described so far, in practice, the differences in operation between universities and companies are substantial.

The discussion of the TCM emphasised its recent emergence as a result of government legislation affecting the universities, and enhanced transparency on the part of the HEFCs concerning their funding methodologies. The innocent cargo cult previously prevalent among academics is giving way to a more sophisticated linking of activity and financial support. Such staff have not generally chosen their profession, however, for the opportunity to practise as amateur accountants and are inclined to kick vigorously against the financial goads, particularly that of teaching assessment.

My experience in the USA suggests that the problem is environmental rather than genetic, and that UK academics are well able to master the financial intricacies of securing external funding as an irksome but routine component of their professional activities. Even so, they will continue to be insulated from the pressure familiar to companies to satisfy shareholders with dividends and capital appreciation.

Figure 2 (page 154) offers a clue to a profound difference between university and company operations: universities are characterised by a bewildering labyrinth of committees, subcommittees, working groups and task forces that proliferate at Council, Senate, Faculty and Department levels, and exercise legislative, administrative, advisory, judicial, negotiating and liaison functions. Why?

This complex committee system derives from the intensity of specialisation of professional expertise and its consequent wide differentiation among academic departments, even within the same Faculty. This can all too easily lead to departmental operation as isolated baronial fiefdoms. Committees facilitate communication and co-operation between departments, and across intellectual divides. They serve as a managerial mechanism to mediate the often conflicting constraints of synergy and opportunities of empowerment. In practice, vice-chancellors have negligible formal power, and little more authority, within their universities. They have, however, enormous influence and potential for leadership through their pervasive presence within, and skilled use of, the committee system to initiate and to advance or impede developments selectively.

The conflicts epitomised by 'the prisoner's dilemma' are aggravated in universities by the fact that academics may be strongly affiliated with the 'invisible college' represented by their professional interests, ie the relevant network of scholars and researchers around the world who communicate with each other, and recognise each other's achievements by invitations to conferences, elections to professional societies, awards of prizes, etc.

Within the Maslow hierarchy of needs, 'survival' and 'security' are assured in the university by powerful formal and informal mechanisms which generally protect employment to retirement for academic staff other than those on probationary or fixed-term initial appointments. This frees them to achieve the higher satisfactions of 'affiliation', 'esteem' and 'self-fulfilment'. As far as their university is concerned, it is my observation that both UK and US academics consider their primary affiliation as being with their department (or even with a group within it, if it is large); they are only weakly coupled to their Faculty, and even less so to the university in general. Particularly for their research, their access to esteem is primarily via the invisible colleges; their affiliations with colleagues and organisations outside their universities are correspondingly strong, and offer manifold off-campus opportunities for the exercise of professional leadership and for self-fulfilment.

Under such circumstances, the promotion of synergy within a university is likely to be even more complex than in a company, where job security is limited and individual needs of the workforce for affiliation, esteem and self-fulfilment can be satisfied primarily within it. This is reflected in the complexity of the committee system referred to earlier; one of its functions is to determine what represents synergy, and the university's best interests, when both on-campus and invisible-college activities are taken into account.

I have already defined the basic steps required towards organisational improvement. In universities, the vice-chancellor is formally responsible for ensuring that such steps are taken, generally by delegation to individuals and via the complex committee system. For example, the academic portfolio of the university - its disciplinary mix and specific teaching or research programmes - is subject to Senate approval. In practice, however, the committee system has to contend with the fiercely-defended independence characteristic of academics. It has its origins in the reasonable (but debatable) proposition that the individual academic is best able to determine what to do, and how to do it, in his or her professional research and teaching. This proposition is supplemented by the further (also debatable) principle that academics should always be free to express heterodox opinions.

If such notions of academic freedom were accepted, they must be, however, circumscribed to some extent to reflect the individual's membership of the university, and derivation of support from it (not the least of which is pay). The university has the right and responsibility to safeguard its collective, long-term objectives against individual self-interest and short-termism, and its reputation against the unconstrained expression of ideas. To balance such tensions, university committees typically legislate and administer at three levels: those of principles, guidelines and rules.

Principles effectively express the university's desired ethos: what perfection would be like, if it could be approached in its dealings with students, staff and the external environment. By their nature, such lofty ideals, typically enshrined in Charters, need to be supplemented by practical guidelines to provide advice on what consti- tutes desirable conduct and favourable directions for development. Inevitably, some precise rules must be defined to constrain undesirable actions, and to prescribe consistent procedures necessary in such areas as student admission and graduation, the recruitment and welfare of staff, responsible accounting for funds, the construction and renovation of buildings, and accurate projection of the university's corporate identity in the outside world.

There are undoubtedly cases of lone scholars or re- searchers doggedly pursuing unpopular lines over extended periods whose results or interpretations are finally trium- phantly vindicated. Such cases loom large in university folklore, but in my experience occur only rarely. Most often, lines are unpopular for good reason, and prove unsound or relatively unproductive; progress is made mostly by sound, determined scholars and researchers who are occasionally fortunate enough to open up an unusually rich vein of knowledge. Nevertheless, universities typically organise themselves with minimal rule-based constraints on individual academics, and rely on their professionalism and local leadership within loosely-defined principles and guidelines to optimise their contributions to university-wide objectives.

Unfortunately, a system which caters well for occasional geniuses (who will probably emerge, anyway, even from locations as improbable as the Berne Patent Office), and for the very good or outstanding, may be overgenerous to the much more numerous mediocre minds, and be susceptible to exploitation by the inadequate and the slothful. Its vulnerability is most evident in scholarship and research. The invisible college, for example, provides as much opportunity for protracted, unproductive absences from campus for inveterate globetrotters as it offers creative stimulation to ready, active minds. We have probably all met a few academics who patronise the university that pays them as if they were generously donating their time to a voluntary organisation.

The relatively weak accountability of academics for the productive exercise of their freedom would be intolerable in a company, and it is only recently that the pressure of HEFC research and teaching assessments has focused university attention on the balance between freedom and accountability. It is noteworthy that the ex-polytechnics, which are more oriented towards teaching than the older universities, typically exercise tighter contractual constraints on their academic staff.

## *How the university and the company are converging*

The intensity of specialisation of professional expertise in universities strongly inhibits lateral communication and co-operation across them, and the satisfaction of individual need for affiliation, esteem and self-fulfilment is often dependent on off-campus invisible colleges. A prime factor in the evolution of the elaborate committee system typical of universities is that it serves to mitigate the difficulty of optimising university-wide operation, particularly resource generation, allocation and utilisation. It should properly be slow and ponderous when decisions are taken concerning staff appointments that may endure for thirty years, or in endorsing academic programmes that may take a decade to plan, initiate and phase out, if they are unsuccessful, but it is poorly adapted to the faster-moving, post-Jurassic period in which universities now find themselves. When concentrated effort required, working groups are helpful; when a decision is required before a deadline, task forces are most effective.

If lateral communication and co-operation are difficult in universities, so too are vertical management and communication up and down the organisational structure: domains of knowledge, and the techniques by which teaching, learning, scholarship and research are conducted, can change so radically over periods as short as a few years to a decade, that the promotion of those in the most senior academic ranks may have depended on performance in fields that are no longer of prime importance, or are simply irrelevant to the managerial activities of a head of department, dean, pro-vice-chancellor, or vice-chancellor. Such senior staff may understand neither the professional expertise of those whom they are managing, nor the materials, methods, and technology that they utilise. Their lateral and vertical spans of expertise and effective management may be so limited that the delegation of authority to act, ie progressively increased empowerment, is forced upon them.

Universities have spent centuries coping with the organisational problems of disparate, highly-specialised professional activities by promoting distributed local academic leadership in preference to rigid, hierarchical management. The provocative underlying question is effectively, 'Why do we need academic managers?' It is a legitimate question, often formulated rhetorically by exasperated academics; the analogous question is often expressed stridently in the National Health Service. As evidenced by the universities, a balanced set of processes operated in an organisation growing and evolving organically, whose leadership is diffused throughout a flexible managerial structure, is manifestly a plausible alternative model.

In an increasingly knowledge-intensive world, companies are experiencing the same managerial problem of rapidly-increasing professional complexity, rendering lateral and vertical communication and organisation increasingly difficult. There can be few executive directors, for example, who could carry out the roles through which they were promoted, say, five to ten years ago, using the processes by which they are now conducted, without re-training. It is not surprising to find recent management literature wrestling with the problems of delayering, empowerment and its concomitant needs for continuing education and training, new integrative mechanisms such as TQM and process re-engineering, and new organisational models, typically involving contractual rather than lifetime employment, and the buying in, rather than internal development, of highly specialised expertise. Since universities have always had these problems, even if now intensified by rapid change, companies may be able to learn from their experiences.

By now, my academic, industrial and commercial colleagues will be equally apprehensive about the conclusions towards which I have been leading them. Universities are becoming increasingly aware that their invisible colleges effectively determine their funding through their peer review roles in research and teaching assessments. Their sensitivity to the marketplace, and the influences of the various stakeholders in it, is being rapidly enhanced and becoming company-like. At the same time, companies are experiencing rapidly-intensifying problems in managing optimally a highly-specialised professional workforce. This may well lead to a softening of rigid, multi-layered managerial structures in favour of more university-like operation.

The central question is how the 'committee' systems in universities and companies will develop and converge to overcome inertia, inadequately-informed decision-making and organisation-wide suboptimality. In both, the rapid obsolescence of current expertise, and the emergence of new fields of sophisticated knowledge on which competitive success will depend, will inevitably challenge the principle of lifetime employment, though EU legislation is progressively constraining companies in the reshaping of their workforce.

'Perish the thought' may say both sides vehemently, but universities and companies **are** converging under similar influences on many aspects of their organisation and operation. As a vice-chancellor, I can only hope not to be crushed between them, or by the rhetorical violence that these modest speculations may provoke!

# CLINTON SILVER

*On Leadership*

---

Clinton Silver CBE CIMgt joined Marks & Spencer in
1952 after university and National Service. He spent his
entire career with the retailing giant and served under all
the company's chairmen from Simon Marks to Richard
Greenbury. He joined the company's board in 1978,
became joint managing director in 1990 and deputy
chairman in 1991. He retired from the company in July
1994 and is now an advisor. He is on the board of
Hillsdown Holdings, the Pentland Group, Tommy Hil-
figer Corporation and is chairman of the British Fashion
Council. He is a companion of the Institute of Management and of the Textile Institute. He was awarded the
CBE in 1993.

Clinton Silver is chairman of the Israel/Diaspora Trust,
chairman of the Jewish Association for Business Ethics,
deputy chairman of the board of governors of Caldicott
School, member of the appeal board at Southampton
University and member of the Board of Youth and Music.

The principles which permeate Marks and Spencer were established by Simon Marks and Israel Sieff. They transformed a small business which began life as a stall in Leeds market into the UK's most profitable retail chain. But, the growth of M&S cannot be measured solely in financial terms, although its reputation is inextricably linked to its financial success. The company name is synonymous with quality, value and fair dealing. Simon and Israel built up close relationships with suppliers and an intimate understanding of the goods. This approach which was initially applied to apparel and later to foods, enabled the company to revolutionise both industries in the UK. Partnership relationships with suppliers are something of a vogue currently. They have been practised by Marks and Spencer for at least sixty years.

Success does not come by accident. There is no formula and what works for one company cannot necessarily be transported to another and expected to repeat its success. Businesses evolve differently and develop their own personalities and principles. You can compete by aiming to be the cheapest in the street or through the quality of your products and service. One way is not necessarily 'better' than the other, but they are addressing different markets which will imbue the respective organisations with different emphases.

The culture of the business pervades the attitude and performance of everyone within Marks and Spencer. This is not a theory but a fact of business life. Not to understand it, or seek to understand it, is the sure route to commercial failure.

M&S does not have a formal mission statement. Its objectives are satisfying customers and making a profit for shareholders. However, fulfilling this aim is made possible by the ethos of the company, which is based on the simple idea of treating people decently whether they are employees, suppliers, customers or members of the local community. Interestingly, M&S often receives praise for being decent and honourable, as if such behaviour is unusual and unexpected. In fact it is an important advantage in a highly commercial and profit-centred business.

Treating people fairly and decently does not imply that the company is soft or sloppy. Good human relations are good business. This is a fact which is increasingly acknowledged. Companies now seek to involve their employees directly in the running of the business; and acknowledge their broader responsibilities for the environment and society.

I have dwelt on the company and its principles. It is a grave error to confuse practices with principles. While working within the principles, every practice must be questioned constantly, and the company given the positive leadership which enables it to develop, adapt, change and grow.

### 'Knowledge itself is power'

The starting point for any manager must be the organisation he or she is leading. The leader must understand the business in detail and relish it. In business, effective leadership is built on this understanding.

Everyone at M&S knows that the chairman and other directors visit stores constantly talking to sales floor staff, management and customers. You cannot pay lip service to understanding the organisation you lead: top managers work hard for long hours.

Everyday contact is important because of the need to have a grasp of detail. Broad brush leadership is not effective. Managers must have detailed understanding of every part of the business and they must be merchants. They must be experts in their products or services, and understand their customers. Corporate leaders cannot create realistic strategies for a business if they do not understand fundamentally the market they are serving.

People watch the leader. You should not seek to establish clones, but must remember that in every aspect of your behaviour, you are setting standards for more junior colleagues who are ambitious.

### 'To be discontented with the divine discontent'

Managers need to know the details of how their business operates so that they can see how it can be improved.

This is not an occasional exercise, but a continuous one. Leaders must probe at grass roots level, ask questions, and listen to the answers.

Managing by Walking Around has been a feature of M&S for as long as I can remember. When I joined M&S in 1952, Simon Marks was constantly visiting stores and head office departments to understand the business concerns of his staff and their ideas. He constantly called for 'divine discontent' from his executives. He meant that they should never be satisfied. Never. Whatever you are doing now, can be improved, dealt with more efficiently, changed or even eliminated. Good leaders are intolerant of events because they are continually asking how the business can be better run. Especially when things are going well they must question policy.

*'Tell me, and I will forget; show me, and I may remember; involve me, and I will understand'*

At M&S there is a culture of communication. This does not mean working by committee, but talking (and listening) to each other. We want people to learn so that they can understand and communicate to others inside and outside the company. For this reason, we are committed to technology - whether it is in textiles, food, operations, administration or finance. Technology provides information, the vital fuel of understanding.

Leaders must work as part of the team, rather than distant figureheads, and be participative, communicating and teaching on the job so that everyone understands what they are doing and how they are contributing to the success of the business.

Does this sound matter of fact? It is. But, leaders have to be excited by the details of their business, no aspect of it should be boring. This enables them to excite and inspire others. Paying attention to the details has made many businesses into success stories. McDonalds' product is not original, but the environment it created is. McDonalds standardised its deliveries and created a clean, welcoming environment. It pays attention to detail and bears in mind the warning of its founder, Ray Kroc: 'Nothing recedes like success.'

## 'Knowing where you want to go is not so difficult as knowing how to get there'

Amid these commonplace issues, lies the inspiration for visionary leadership. Vision means being able to look beyond your immediate business and form a view on new opportunities; it is not developed in ivory towers. Nor can it be separated from practical experience.

M&S has a reputation for steadiness, but has been driven forward constantly by the practical realisation of visionary thinking. The development of a unique food business; the introduction of homeware; the development of city centre 'departmental' stores; the creation of out of town stores; going abroad - we were developing in France before the UK joined the Common Market, and now trade in Spain, Holland, Belgium, North America and the Far East; the M&S shopping card; a new business in financial services; an unrivalled IT system.

After the vision, getting it done is the test of management fibre and tenacity.

The successful leader needs commercial judgement. This presupposes a basic level of intelligence - something you don't suddenly discover at a business school. Intelligence needs to be blended with wisdom and an ability to analyse the issues involved. Decisions are best made on the basis of an understanding of the facts - they are not bravura acts of machismo. Having made a decision you must stand by it. You cannot lead with uncertainty or equivocation, and you must have a clear plan of what you believe needs to be done to transfer ideas into action. Equally, when things go wrong, the leader has to be the first person to admit to the misjudgement and, throwing aside the failed policy, start again.

The bottom line for any leader must be his or her ability to make an impact. You have to be able to make things happen, which comes from an inner strength which many contenders for leadership do not have. Making things happen implies that people want to listen to what you have to say, and this, in good measure, depends on your having been a good listener.

It is also useful to have style. Style separates the great leaders and gives them a unique ability to communicate effectively. A good leader must demonstrate a stable personality and must not suffer from violent swings of mood. He or she must also have a certain amount of detachment without being aloof, but staff, suppliers and customers have to be aware of an active involvement. The leader has to possess integrity and it must show. In a word, the leader has to embody everything that the organisation stands for and aspires to.

### 'You may not desist from participating in the task, but no-one is given the opportunity to finish it'

You can do great things in a business. People like Simon Marks created organisations which have stood the test of time. But, people pass, and for anyone in business the final judgement is how they have developed their heirs.

William Hewlett, the co-founder of Hewlett-Packard said: 'As I look back on my life's work, I'm probably most proud of having helped to create a company that by virtue of its values, practices and success has had a tremendous impact on the way companies are managed around the world. And I'm particularly proud that I am behind an ongoing organisation that can live on as a role model long after I'm gone.'

Leadership has failed when it carries on into old age simply through lack of trust in those who follow. Perhaps, then, the most important task of leadership is to develop people, to recognise strengths and weaknesses, to criticise but not to condemn, to encourage success through delegation and empowerment. It is only through mobilising the strengths and ideas of people that any leader, and any organisation, can succeed.

# TOM FARMER

*On Leadership*

---

*Tom Farmer* CBE CIMgt *is chairman and chief executive of Kwik-Fit Holdings plc.*

Tom Farmer opened his first business, Tyres & Accessory Supplies in 1964 in Buccleuch Street, Edinburgh. In 1970 he 'retired' to America, but returned in 1971 to establish Kwik-Fit. The group now has a turnover of £300 million, operates through nearly 800 locations in the UK, Ireland, Holland and Belgium, and employs over 5,000 people.

Tom Farmer is chairman of Scottish Business in the Community, Chairman of Investors in People Scotland and a board member of Investors in People UK.

'The manager administers; the leader innovates. The manager maintains; the leader develops. The manager relies on systems; the leader relies on people. The manager counts on controls; the leader counts on trust. The manager does things right; the leader does the right thing,' says the American leadership guru, Warren Bennis. The differences between managers and leaders seem to highlight turning points in the development of Kwik-Fit and its 5,000 employees.

Innovation and development, require first class management, but ultimately they must stem from the leader. For it is the leader who is either complacent about the standing of the business, or who is impatient to see it grow. It is the leader's function to provide the long-term strategic thinking for managers to implement. It is the leader who sets the atmosphere and philosophy for the way in which the organisation treats and develops its people. It is the leader who nurtures the trust that the business puts in people and develops in them, so that trust becomes the core of their own business philosophy. And, at Kwik-Fit, this is supported by an emphasis on customer care, service, training and education and communications. These themes are among the most important which leaders must develop in their strategic thinking for quality management to implement.

In the 21 years in which Kwik-Fit has operated - and its auto centres can now be found throughout the UK as well as in Ireland, Holland and Belgium - I have always been a hands-on chief executive. A business, any business, needs leadership and its leader requires a philosophy by which he or she guides it.

Kwik-Fit's philosophy was first expressed in 1971. In the company's first annual report to shareholders I wrote: 'At Kwik-Fit the most important person is the customer, and it must be the aim of us all the give 100 per cent satisfaction 100 per cent of the time. The managers and staff at our centres are the all-important contact with the customers, and they are the key to the success of the Kwik-Fit Group.'

### Going beyond slogans

Customers come first. If there are no customers there is no business. This is so obvious that I can never understand how some companies forget it - and some of them are giants in their field.

Looking after customers, caring for them, has now become one of the most popular themes in business. But it must be more than an advertising slogan. It must be enshrined in the company's philosophy otherwise it is a meaningless marketing gimmick - and the customer can soon tell which it is. Service as a theme involves everyone who works in a company and it can only operate effectively if the company invests in training its people so that they really understand that the customer comes first. The main asset of a business is its human resource, the people who work in a company and for it.

Training creates the environment in which the people who work in the business understand how to make progress in their careers by 'doing it right' and doing it right first time.

Work done expertly, leading to customer delight, does two things: it satisfies the craving of the human ego for doing something well rather than badly; and it saves having to do the job again. Retail has been defined as selling things which don't come back, to customers who do. In Kwik-Fit the things are goods and services, all of which are the best quality for the price. They represent excellent value for money.

Financial value is only one part of the equation. Kwik-Fit's original mission statement talked of '100 per cent customer satisfaction'. We have now changed that to '100 per cent customer delight'. Satisfied customers have only been given what they expected. That is no longer enough. We have to go the extra mile and give something that is not expected. Customers who are delighted with their purchases not only come back again but tell their friends. All Kwik-Fit people understand that their function is to delight their customers. We believe that it is the best way to continue to make progress and perhaps it is the only way to survive.

It makes obvious business sense. If everyone is selling goods at the same price you have to find other ways of being different - of adding value for the customers. That inevitably comes down to interpersonal relationships -

how the person serving you relates to you. The real strength of an organisation lies in constantly monitoring and evaluating its customer service and, when things go wrong, rectifying them quickly. A complaining customer is the greatest opportunity we have to convert into a loyal - and delighted - customer. We have to listen to complaints without interruption and guarantee a speedy solution. That is why we give out reply-paid questionnaires with receipts and have a special freephone helpline which is open round the clock. We acknowledge every response and act upon it.

Kwik-Fit is different because it employs different management practices. Major competitors probably follow what Tom Peters and Robert Waterman called the 'numerative, rationalised approach to management that dominates the business schools'. This is mechanical and inflexible. We prefer Peter Drucker's contrasting view that 'management is... what used to be called liberal art: liberal because it deals with the fundamentals of knowledge, self-know-ledge, wisdom and leadership; art because it is practice and application'.

But how do you achieve the application? How do you get people to give that bit extra - to give delight rather than simply satisfaction?

For both customers and staff to 'understand' requires a communication programme. Modern techniques of communication have made communication with customers and potential customers easy, if expensive. Providing the promise is never greater than the reality then, by and large, the plethora of methods work.

As to the people who work in the business, it is still true that the most effective form of communication is face-to-face and, since Kwik-Fit is a network of small businesses which together create a large one, this is the method we prefer. At Kwik-Fit we operate the management philosophy of 'Walk the Talk'. It is obvious that personal communication is cheap, efficient and gives feedback. And

with that goes being able to have a frank discussion at whatever staff or management level. It is the best way of clearing the air.

One of the biggest problems in management today is the inability to look someone in the eye and say, 'Look, can we just have an easy, open discussion and I'll tell you exactly what I think and you can do the same?' There is nothing wrong with telling someone they are not doing the job well. They are probably unhappy and there is usually a reason. You've got to catch a situation before it becomes too critical. Now, this sort of face-to-face communication is supplemented by a massive investment in continuous training, in our own training schools; in information technology; in a specialised incentive scheme.

To achieve customer delight we must provide proper education through training and ensuring that our people recognise that the company cares. We cannot expect our people to treat customers any better than they themselves are treated by the company. All our people are my customers and we cannot expect our people to deliver excellent service to the customer if we don't deliver the same to them. Kwik-Fit is, for example, part of the Investors in People standard. This is based on four key principles:

- ◆ commitment to developing people to achieve business goals and targets

- ◆ reviewing regularly the training and development needs of all people in the context of the business

- ◆ taking relevant action to meet those needs from recruitment throughout people's employment

- ◆ evaluating outcomes for the organisation of training and development as a basis for continuous improvement.

People are critical. Our TV advertising slogan is 'You can't get better than a Kwik-Fit fitter'. It raises the company's profile and promotes its ethos in the market place. But, equally importantly, it also builds confidence within the company and bestows a sense of pride and belonging among our people. Clearly, achieving such pride and a feeling of belonging is not simply achieved by an advertising campaign. It is achieved by leadership built on trust, acceptance of responsibility, shared values and knowledge that the customer is king.

# LEADERSHIP LESSONS

The leaders featured in this book are drawn from the worlds of business, the armed services and the civil service. The range of their backgrounds, occupations and preoccupations is testament to the all-embracing nature of leadership. Their approaches, ideas and experiences differ wildly; but, nevertheless, there is no doubting the fact that they are leaders. And, herein lies the danger of leadership. Leadership constantly runs the risk of being all things to all people; a nebulous catch-all phrase. How can the leadership skills of someone such as England rugby captain, Will Carling, be equated or even compared to those of explorer, John Blashford-Snell, the Prime Minister or the chief executive of a company? The people in this book would contend that the skills of leadership can not only be compared, but are in many cases similar or even identical.

Though personal perspectives and experiences are different, there is certainly a great deal of common ground among the leaders. This is perhaps best summed up by Sir Colin Marshall: 'Leadership is an amalgam of many different facets - vision, dedication and drive - and an array of others. They are rarely found in one person. Yet, while the individual characteristics of a leader vary from person to person, there are common foundations:

you have to be respected by those you are going to lead;
you need to be a good communicator, willing and able to
stand at the front of the organisation; and people must
be prepared to follow you.'

These 'Leadership Lessons' bring the views and opinions of the featured leaders together and attempt to make
sense of them under the broad - and forever broadening
- concept of leadership. It is not a blueprint for leadership. Indeed, the leaders make it abundantly clear that
leadership is constantly in a state of evolution and flux.

General Sir Peter Inge identifies this as a vital element
in leadership - 'The fact that leadership, like other forms
of behaviour, continually evolves is a healthy thing. You
don't find static leaders. They, too, move and develop
to fit changing circumstances. To do so requires enormous self-awareness and self-discipline. The latter is a
critical factor in the armed forces where the emphasis is
not, as many believe, on enforced discipline, although
that has a part, but on self-discipline.'

Some attributes are often left unspoken. Leadership
takes huge reservoirs of energy, both physical and mental.
Sir David Gillmore recalls the exhausting pace set by
Margaret Thatcher, writing speeches through the night
and rising at dawn to begin work again. 'The leader has
to project consistent optimism, confidence and strength
of purpose. Such commodities do not come cost-free and
will, over time, drain reserves of energy,' admits Richard
Wells. 'The leader - at all levels - needs strong personal

support mechanisms. Inner strength and confidence will be essential and will grow at different paces and in different directions according to the rigours of the moment.'

Leadership remains a potent combination of individualism within an organisational framework. As such, it will always defy formulaic approaches to making it work more successfully. As Peter Drucker observes: 'There is no recipe for success, only failure.'

### Are managers leaders?

There is one crucial area where the leaders tend to disagree: the relationship between management and leadership. To some, the two are inextricably interlinked to the point that the difference should be indistinguishable. To others, the difference between management and leadership must be distinguishable; they are mutually exclusive.

'Management is a purely mechanistic thing,' says Sir Raymond Lygo. 'It can be dealt with through balance sheets, as far as finance is concerned and through the management chain, as long as the organisation and manning of the structure is logical. In other words, you could almost place management in the hands of a computer to create the best network for the organisation, the most logical and straightforward structure, and the ratios and checks required to ensure that all is proceeding according to plan.'

The separation of management and leadership is borne out by looking at articles on the subjects of leadership and strategy, one of the principle activities of senior managers. A single run through of a database found 17,076 articles on strategy; 2,344 on leadership and a mere 49 which mentioned both strategy and leadership. Yet, even the most ardent strategist would be likely to agree that leadership is a key factor in converting strategy into action.

190

The nature of the divide between the two is mapped out further by Sir Raymond Lygo. While management is a science (something built around hard facts and measurable results), Lygo believes that leadership is an art (creative, intangible and abstract) - 'Leadership derives its strength from the humanities. It is an exercise in inculcating the managerial process with humanity. As such, leadership stands alone but not separate from management. You can have excellent leadership qualities while not being a capable manager.' Lygo's argument is that management is formulaic while leadership can never be so prescriptive.

In a similar vein, General Sir Peter Inge regards leadership as the dominant partner: 'Please do no think that I am denigrating management, but I believe that man management is a facet of leadership.'

The most forceful voice against such a separation comes from Sir Peter Parker. 'I resist strongly the dichotomy sometimes made between management and leading. Managing means leading, making things happen through people. That is relevant at every level of management, not just the profiled personalities at the top.'

Perhaps the reasoned middle ground is the observation by Valerie Strachan that 'leadership is a human science'. As such it is prone to the vicissitudes of humanity while, at the same time, being precisely defined enough to allow certain skills to be learned and developed.

---

### Managers and leaders

To leadership guru, Warren Bennis, leadership is a skill which can be learned by the manager willing to put in substantial effort. It is, however, fundamentally different from management. 'To survive in the 21st century we're going to need a new generation of leaders, not managers. The distinction is an important one. Leaders conquer the context - the volatile, turbulent, ambiguous surroundings that sometimes seek to conspire against us and will surely suffocate us if we let them - while managers surrender to it.'

He goes on to list the fundamental differences between managers and leaders as:

- the manager administers; the leader innovates

- the manager is a copy; the leader is an original

- the manager maintains; the leader develops

♦ the manager focuses on systems and structure; the leader focuses on people

♦ the manager relies on control; the leader inspires trust

♦ the manager has a short-range view; the leader has a long-range perspective

♦ the manager asks how and when; the leader asks what and why

♦ the manager has his eye on the bottom line; the leader has his eye on the horizon

♦ the manager accepts the status quo; the leader challenges it

♦ the manager is the classic good soldier; the leader is his own person

♦ the manager does things right; the leader does the right thing.[1]

## The irresistible lure of leadership

The management-leadership debate will undoubtedly continue. It is ridden with paradoxes which, in the main, appear unbridgeable. Yet, it is an addictive debate. Quite clearly, the leaders - and many others - have a fascination with the concept and practice of leadership.

They are interested in leadership - but not in the same way as a barrister is interested in the law. They want to understand and at the same time admit that a true understanding of all the intricacies of leadership is probably beyond any one person. Churchill was a great leader, but did he understand what made him a great leader? Probably not.

Though personal recognition of how leadership works is immensely difficult, leaders agree on the *need* for leadership. In a famous 1977 *Harvard Business Review* article, American academic Abraham Zaleznik noted that we have 'a need for competent managers and a longing for great leaders'. The longing remains.

'Leadership is as important now as it has ever been, and is necessary in all levels of an organisation. Undoubtedly certain changes mean that leadership has become more difficult and complex and is more in the public gaze. However, perhaps great leaders will continue to exercise these challenges through their moral courage,' says General Sir Peter Inge.

No matter what the organisation, or the group of people involved, the leaders argue that leadership is something we constantly look for. 'Leadership is the quality we all hope to find in those who are in some way "in charge", whether in the private or the public sector,' says Valerie Strachan. 'A real leader, I think, is easy to recognise. He or she is the one who guesses the future right, who can see what is needed to keep the organisation going - and going forward - and who can, most importantly, convince everyone in the organisation to follow his or her lead. While such skills are easy to recognise, they are notoriously difficult to achieve.'

We know it when we see it, but pigeon-holing leaders and the characteristics of leadership is all but impossible. Leaders are the same, but different. It is the areas of difference and distinction which are notoriously difficult to pin-down. 'Leaders often possess a modicum of eccentricity,' points out Sir David Gillmore. 'Their eccentricity is endearing rather than off-putting. Clearly, this is not something you can create, but it does mark out from the crowd leaders like Churchill and de Gaulle.'

It is the very elusiveness of leadership which appears to make it attractive and alluring. 'The sheer idea of leadership reminds us of the sheer humanity of management, the mystery, the charisma,' says Sir Peter Parker. 'We find ourselves enjoying the scope to speculate about leadership, and how it happens. Is it education or lack of it, sensitivity or insensitivity? Will, guts or just wanting money very, very much? I find that there are no absolutes, no models.'

The abstract world is not one normally inhabited by successful business people or civil servants. Their currency is results, achievements, facts and figures. Leadership is acknowledged as a vital ingredient in achieving results. Leadership enables an organisation to make full use of its resources. It is a commercial weapon, one vividly mapped out by Sir Colin Marshall: 'The role of leadership is especially important in a service business. If morale is low then you simply can't deliver customer service. That is what a service business is all about. Leaders inspire an organisation and take responsibility for creating the essential motivation to move things forward, constantly improve and meet objectives. Excellence in leadership is a prerequisite for business success.'

Leadership is recognised by the leaders as intangible, but critical; a constant in a changeable world. There is no formula, only the strength, wisdom and personality of the individual. 'Leadership is intensely personal and it has to remain open to individual interpretations,' says General Sir Peter Inge.

Interestingly, there is little insistence by the leaders that leadership is - or ever was - the preserve of a chosen few. Leadership is not elitist, but wide ranging. 'Leadership is not solely the domain of military leaders, great politicians or of business people. It is found in all aspects of our lives and all aspects of our working lives, no matter what our job or where we carry it out,' observes Sir David Gillmore. 'In fact, like many people, I have found that leadership has impinged and played a part at virtually every stage of my life and career. Teaching in the 1960s in a school in inner-city London, I was confronted with situations which required leadership.'

## *Who is a leader?*

If leadership is omnipresent, the logical conclusion is that we are all leaders now - or, at least, are exercising leadership to some extent or having it exercised upon us. The tentacles of leadership are spreading. It is a trend noted by Valerie Strachan as she remembers the early part of her career where her 'awareness of leadership depended entirely on how close I was to the centre of the action. I suspect that this rule applied throughout the civil service'. Now, leadership no longer depends on being near to the epicentre of the organisation. Instead, the practice of effective leadership affects us all.

Within organisations, leadership is no longer the sole preserve of a coterie of senior executives. Research comparing the work of Hewlett Packard product managers in 1970 and 1985 found that the 1980s manager was:

- overseeing more changeable product lines

- operating within a context of continuously developing technology

- having to produce to ever-increasing quality standards

- spending half his or her time on setting direction, communicating the need for change and motivating employees.

A decade later, it is likely that the product managers will be having to carry out many more roles once regarded as containing leadership skills. The product manager is now as much a leader as the chief executive. The context is different, as are the skills required, but leadership must still be exercised.

Even though the practice of leadership is becoming more widely dispersed, there is a fear - a very British fear - of proclaiming yourself a leader. It smacks, some would say, of arrogance. A leader, after all, remains synonymous with Churchill - someone in the public eye, facing identifiable foes - rather than someone managing a company or running a civil service department. Many have qualms about being thought of, and thinking of themselves, as leaders.

For some, leadership comes with the job. For others, leadership *is* the job. BA's Sir Colin Marshall says: 'As chairman of British Airways I am in a position where leadership is required, indeed it is expected from me. That is how I am perceived and how I see myself. To Sir Colin, providing leadership is part of his job description. As understanding and appreciation of leadership increases, it seems likely that such recognition of the pivotal role of leadership will become more commonplace. Perhaps in the future executives will even have the word leader on their business cards.

## Role models

Who do leaders look to for inspiration? Not surprisingly, the role models cited by the leaders are a disparate group - from Field-Marshals to successful executives. Yet, military role models predominate.

The power of military role models is simply explained by Sir Peter Parker: 'Of course, war and even Cold War, make life dramatically simple. In business the parameters of leadership are less clear. There are no King's or Queen's Regulations to hold the line; there are no Regimental Sergeant-Majors with booming voices to put the inefficient on a charge. Managerial power is also fundamentally a contrast to uniformed power. And to political power - managers are not elected by those they manage; they can make no claim to the sovereignty of the people. While there may be many lords in the boardrooms, only very few claim a divine right of management.' In warfare the parameters, aspirations and expectations are crystal clear. They have to be. Leadership is the same, but the rules are different.

It is perhaps surprising that military and historical figures continue to loom so large. Sir David Gillmore, for example, cites Nelson's ability to motivate his crews for long periods in the face of adversity. The most obvious explanation must be that the characteristics of great leaders are timeless. Also, many of the leaders included in this book have had direct contact with some of the most imposing and successful leaders of our time.

Personal experience - meeting and dealing with great leaders - is crucial. Sir Peter Parker talks of the impact of Lord Mountbatten and Field-Marshall Slim on his perception of leadership. Slim, mentioned by others, remains a somewhat neglected leadership luminary.

Interestingly, the leaders rarely look to fellow executives for leadership inspiration. One of the exceptions is Sir Colin Marshall who cites fellow executives Don Petrie and Harold Geneen as crucial shaping influences on his thinking. Geneen, in particular, is as far from the glamorous, action-oriented, military ideal as can be imagined. His business leadership cannot be questioned, but as an inspiration he plainly falls into a quite different category from the likes of Mountbatten and Slim with their motivational talks in war-torn jungles.

## What makes a leader?

### 1. Are leaders born?

The question of whether leadership is an innate gift which cannot be taught has occupied generations of thinkers. Today's leaders appear unhindered by philosophical contemplation. They are pragmatic - yes, some leaders are created with their gifts already fully formed, but the majority have to work hard at developing the skills of leadership.

'Leadership requires mastery of a myriad of techniques. To this, leaders must bring a wide variety of natural attributes and some kind of inspirational ability. Techniques can be learned, but the other elements defy conventional training and, to a large extent, precise definition,' says Sir David Gillmore. 'The great leaders bring a wide range of natural attributes to the techniques they have acquired and the tasks they face. They are likely to possess intelligence, integrity, commitment and courage, among many other traits.'

Sir Colin Marshall adds: 'I believe that leaders aren't simply born with innate leadership skills which are waiting to be discovered, but that leaders can be developed. Indeed, there are more opportunities than ever before for young managers to enhance their knowledge of leadership and develop their practical leadership skills.'

The leaders suggest that there are a plethora of development opportunities - from formal leadership courses to the informal education of experience. Opportunities abound for people to discover and nurture their leadership skills. 'Great leaders inspire and make leadership appear available to all. And, increasingly, leadership - or, at least, the skills it involves - is available,' says Sir David Gillmore. 'While leadership may involve luck and is, to some extent, thrust upon you, it is possible to learn the techniques. There are now a large number of business schools and specialist institutions offering courses, and entire programmes, on the tools and techniques of leadership. The theory is available to all but, by learning it, you don't automatically become a leader.'

Despite their enthusiasm for formal training courses and programmes, the leaders have generally undergone little in the way of formal training themselves. However, it is noticeable that the range of their experience is generally large. Many had leadership roles thrust upon them early in their careers or spent time assembling a portfolio of differing perspectives and experiences. Sir Colin Marshall travelled the world on a liner; Sir David Gillmore moved through a variety of jobs including teaching and working in France; and those in the armed services and civil service were routinely moved from job to job to build up their knowledge and experience.

The leaders give themselves the opportunity to accumulate a range of experiences. They realise - intuitively in most cases - that by putting themselves in different and difficult situations they enable themselves to develop fundamental skills.

*Luck and leadership*

'I want lucky people. The luckier my managers are, the better I like it,' John Moores, founder of the Littlewoods empire, is reputed to have said. And, indeed, luck is a word the leaders often use. 'I have been very fortunate in how my career has developed. I was in the right place at the right time. But it is not all down to luck. Luck goes with success,' reflects Sir Colin Marshall. It is a view echoed by other leaders.

Their timing is impeccable. In his work on high performance managers, Ashridge Management College's Phil Hodgson concludes: 'High performers create situations, or allow themselves to be drawn into situations, where their strengths are needed. They are in the right place at the right time continually, able to escape from the mundanity of non-achievement.'

The leaders ride their luck. They accept that learning and opportunities are often far from systematic. Life and careers are often a matter of chance. You either ride your luck and seize the opportunity or allow it to pass by.

### 2. The human touch

Addressing the superintendents of his factories, the nineteenth century businessman, Robert Owen, said: 'Many of you have long experiences in your manufacturing operations of the advantages of substantial, well-contrived and well-executed machinery. If, then, due care as to the state of the machinery can produce such beneficial results, what may not be expected if you devote equal attention to your animate machines, which are far more wonderfully constructed?'

All the contemporary leaders agree that the human touch is central to any leadership role. Marshalling, motivating and engaging everyone in the organisation is regarded as one of the prime responsibilities of the leader. Says General Sir Peter Inge: 'The leader must understand those he is responsible for as people and as individuals.'

Though in practice it is often ignored or overlooked, succession planning is identified as highly important. The leader must not only provide an active lead in the present, but must plan for the future leadership of the organisation.  This is something which some of the great leaders - from Churchill to Margaret Thatcher - have overlooked.  In doing so, they run the risk of having their legacy tarnished.

'I believe that being sensitive to and understanding people, while still demanding their utmost, is central to effective leadership,' says Sir David Gillmore. 'Selecting talented people and promoting the right people is crucial - the chairman of a large company once told me that the only really useful thing he could do was to choose a good successor.'

Sir Raymond Lygo similarly draws attention to differing perspectives on the importance of training and succession planning.  He reflects that, in the navy systems and structures are geared to developing skills and succession plans so that when people move on - which they do every two or three years - the work will carry on seamlessly. He contrasts this with what he found when taking over at British Aerospace - 'I see no structure, no succession planning and nobody trains anybody for anything.'

Perhaps the most forceful explanation of the impor-tance of succession planning is given by Sir Adrian Cadbury. To him, the leader who neglects those around him or her is failing to exercise leadership. 'True leaders encourage their followers to develop their talents and to grow in stature. They build their successors, so that, in time, their leadership will no longer be needed,' says Cadbury. 'False leaders take away from their followers the ability to decide for themselves; they hold them in thrall and diminish them as people. The tests in essence are simple ones, good leaders grow people, bad leaders stunt them; good leaders serve their followers, bad leaders enslave them.'

204

*How long can a leader be effective?*

People who are highly successful tend to find it extremely hard to acknowledge when their powers begin to wane. Sporting stars notoriously carry on for one more fight, one more race, another tournament, when their skills are rapidly disappearing. Frank Sinatra sings on.

Leaders face similar problems. Winston Churchill was a dynamic war leader, but his period of office during peace-time tarnished rather than enhanced his image and reputation. It is not that their skills vanish overnight, but often the skills which make leaders successful in a particular organisation outlive their usefulness. The charismatic leader who creates a fast growing dynamic organisation is rarely the person to continue to lead it when it becomes a giant multinational.

'Leadership has failed when it carries on into old age simply through lack of trust in those who follow,' says Clinton Silver. 'Perhaps, then the most important task of leadership is to develop people, to recognise strengths and weaknesses, to criticise but not to condemn, to encourage success through delegation and empowerment.'

Indeed, the charismatic leader is now commonly regarded with some scepticism. Peter Drucker acknowledges the importance of authority in management, but suggests that charismatic leaders are often blinkered by an illusion of their own infallibility. Believing themselves infallible, they become inflexible and unable to cope with a changing environment.

It is a phenomenon which Sir Peter Parker has personal experience of. 'Staying with an organisation or in a particular job for too long can diminish what made the leader successful in the first place,' he says. 'You find yourself losing time in defensive talk over past decisions, especially the wrong ones. You lose impetus, look over your shoulder too often, reflecting not renewing, repeating and not refreshing, stroking and not spurring on, purring and not prodding yourself. So, without really noticing, the energy, the nerve and direction dissipate. The time inevitably comes in the career of any leader when you have to allow others the opportunity to take the organisation forward.'

Being aware of the time limitations is an important factor identified by a number of the leaders. For some, like BA's Colin Marshall, it is regarded as something requiring constant vigilance. 'The problem commonly encountered by leaders - in whatever field - is that the length of time they have spent in office leads to them being cut off from reality. As a result, they fail to recognise their faults and mistakes. Leaders have to be wary of longevity,' says Sir Colin, pointing to Robert Townsend's suggestion that no-one should be in one position for more than five years. It is not a view Sir Colin holds, but one which serves as a warning - 'You must watch for signs of egotism and a lack of willingness to acknowledge mistakes'.

Communicating effectively with people within the organisation and stakeholders or affected parties outside it is regarded as a vital means of defying the dangers of egotism. Again Sir Peter Parker points to Mountbatten's ability to 'connect' with people - 'he realised he relied on them to complete his mission effectively'.

In the modern business environment, communication is no longer a rigid, formal process. Instead, it has to be dynamic, powerful and immediate. 'If we can simplify something we will. If we can make it simple we can communicate it easily to our people and people can understand, champion it and endeavour to take an active part on the programme,' said John Cahill when chief executive of BTR. This sort of directness is critical to successful communication.

The leaders recognise that a casual or short conversation with someone is more valuable than a few paragraphs in a company newsletter. 'Communication is a vital part of the leadership role. I get around the organisation. I talk to engineers in the hangars, pilots and crew on the planes and customers. If a member of the cabin crew tells me that one of the passengers isn't happy I talk to him or her,' says Sir Colin Marshall.

In the age of e-mail and the Internet, physical presence is still regarded as essential. 'While personality remains a mystery, 'being there' seems to me the stuff of leadership at every level of managing,' observes Sir Peter Parker.

Marks & Spencer is one organisation which has imbued its entire culture with the idea of being there. 'Everyone at M&S knows that the chairman and other directors visit stores constantly talking to sales floor staff, management and customers,' says Clinton Silver. This serves two purposes - it gives the managers insight into the nitty gritty of the business and sets an important example. Says Silver: 'People watch the leader. You should not seek to establish clones, but must remember that in every aspect of your behaviour, you are setting standards for more junior colleagues who are ambitious.'

Sir David Gillmore takes Nelson as a potent example of the power of 'being there'. 'Nelson proves that you can't lead at a distance. 'It is warm work; and this day may be the last to any of us at a moment. But mark you! I would not be elsewhere for thousands,' he said in the midst of the Battle of Copenhagen. You've got to be deeply involved in the organisation. Commitment is not one way; it has to go down and through the organisation. This requires presence - both physical and inspirational.

*Avoiding isolation*

'Leadership is about a commitment to people,' says Sir Colin Marshall, before issuing the warning, 'People at the top of the organisational hierarchy must have access to people in the workplace. If they don't they quickly become cut off.'

The great leaders appear to avoid becoming isolated with relative, intuitive, ease. Mere mortals have to constantly guard against becoming out of touch.

208

This is the antithesis of the traditional notion of the 'great man' school of leadership in which the leader is, by necessity, an isolated and indomitable figure. Today's leaders are sceptical of retaining an objective distance believing that objectivity runs the risk of aloofness. Instead, they place emphasis on their humanity and accessibility. Leaders are also human and, of course, along with this comes the realisation that they are fallible. 'Subordinates do not have the monopoly of fear, doubt, despair, uncertainty or anger and while they are entitled to look to the leader for courage, certainty, optimism and calm, they are not entitled to trap a boss on an emotional pedestal,' says Richard Wells.

'If you have responsibility for an organisation and the people inside it, then you have to make contact with them. You have to be visible and be seen to be about your business,' says Sir Raymond Lygo. 'When you talk to people they must understand from your conversation that you are human as well as their leader and managing director or chief executive and that you are interested in them as individuals... Goodwill and good human relations is like banking. You put money or goodwill into the account which you have with your people and you build it up so that when there are moments of extreme stress you can draw it down. You cannot, of course, overdraw too often or the goodwill will evaporate, but if your people have faith in you and your concern for them, then often you can overdraw the account and get away with it as long as you restore their fortunes as well as yours as soon as possible. '

209

Interestingly many contemporary business leaders work in partnerships - look at Lord Hanson and Lord White, or Anita and Gordon Roddick. The partnership between Lord King and Sir Colin Marshall during the 1980s is a potent example of how leaders can use colleagues to keep in touch and share the burden. 'Lord King served as a sounding board to me as chief executive and to other senior managers,' explains Marshall. 'Such a sounding board is one of the great things any chief executive must have - and is a role I increasingly try to take on myself. As a chief executive you can become isolated and lonely. You need to constantly guard against this happening.'

The leader does not exercise leadership in a vacuum but must enable others to fulfil their potential and enable themselves to fulfil their own potential through communicating with others inside and outside the organisation.

### 3. Setting direction and building values

The leader needs to carry out a precarious balancing act. He or she has to set the long-term objectives and vision of an organisation, yet has also to 'connect' with people throughout the organisation. There is a perpetual danger of becoming bogged down in minor, localised problems or, at the other extreme, becoming cut off from the lifeblood of the organisation. Harold Macmillan was once asked what was the most difficult thing about being Prime Minister. 'Events, my dear boy, events,' he replied.

The minutiae of business is compulsively attractive. 'Leadership is incredibly demanding and is perpetually creating different challenges, so that it is easy to be overtaken by the immediacy of the work in progress,' reflects Sir David Gillmore. 'Under pressure, exhausted and pressed for a decision, leaders need to make the time to draw breath. They must think about the job, look across the board, set objectives and move people towards them together.'

Sir Adrian Cadbury calls on leaders 'to look beyond the immediate issues and to analyse the future options objectively. The lead - the step ahead - which is the badge of the leader is derived from foresight. Leaders anticipate turning points and foresee the need to change direction before others do. They set a firm course, but sense when a change of course is called for. Leaders who lack the gift of foresight stick blindly to their chosen path, in defiance of changing circumstances'.

In the past, the senior executive was expected to be deeply involved in every aspect of a company's activities. Expectations are changing. 'If the people on the front line really are the keys to our success, then the manager's job is to help those people, the people that they serve,' says Robert Hass, president and chief executive of Levi Strauss. 'That goes against the traditional assumption that the manager is in control. In the past, a manager was expected to know everything that was going on and to be deeply involved in a subordinate's activities.'

To overcome the temptation to become involved in every single decision and activity entails:

◆ **a sense of vision**

'We didn't argue what the computer should be, we all knew what the computer should be. Our job was to go out and make it work,' commented one of the design engineers on the Apple Mackintosh team. Such clarity of purpose is rare - for all the mission statements and visionary exhortations by executives in annual reports.

Peter Drucker cut to the heart of the problem in a comparison of Japanese and Western attitudes. 'One of the greatest differences between the Japanese and Europeans and Americans is that they don't take their mission for granted. They start off with "What are we trying to do?" Not, "How do we do it?"'

Having a mobile, yet clear and committed vision is critical in effective leadership. It unites and enables different teams, departments and individuals to forget their differences and work towards a strong, common goal. It is not a public relations exercise or a derided mission statement pinned on a factory notice board. It is a real and living *raison d'etre*.

Vision is interpreted by Sir Adrian Cadbury as direction: 'It is a sense of direction that we need to keep in mind when assessing leadership. The directional sense of leaders is more important than their powers of leadership and the two attributes do not necessarily go together. ... Many have the desire to lead or the gift of leadership, but fewer, far fewer ... combine them with vision and sound judgement. If you are told that a business is a going concern, it is as well to ascertain for yourself in which direction it is going.'

Cadbury goes on to examine the real role of vision: 'Vision is central to ensuring that everyone in an organisation knows what the goals of the enterprise are and how their particular job contributes to them. In addition, a sense of vision is what inspires people to feel, both that the company's aims are their aims and that they are worthy of achievement. Companies are in business to achieve goals. The leader's task is to determine those goals, to communicate them and to win commitment to them.'

◆ **a broader perspective**

'Any environment, however stimulating in the short-term, is constraining. You have to be able to look over the walls, to look outside for new perspectives, examples and inspirations,' says Sir David Gillmore.

The leaders are perpetually searching for new perspectives, fresh insights, more information and more effective methods of delivering their vision. 'Perhaps it is eccentricity which allows leaders to take an alternative view - though in the jargon of leadership theorising it is called 'vision'. They are constantly able to appreciate and adopt a different, broader, more sensitive or more inspiring perspective on a particular situation or issue,' says Gillmore.

◆ **the ability to build and sustain an organisational culture.**

'I believe that the glue which holds a company together is its beliefs and values, rather than its structures and systems,' observes Sir Adrian Cadbury.

To Cadbury the business leader acts as the coping stone of the organisation, from which its values are continually disseminated. The leader does not, however, set values in corporate tablets of stone. 'The leader's role is to distil them and to instil them. I say distil, because the ability to create values from the top is limited, although they can be only too readily undermined from there, since the maintenance of values depends on example. Leadership involves articulating what the business stands for and acting as the guardian of those values,' says Cadbury.

It is a point picked up by Richard Wells who observes: 'The leader is obliged to set standards and insist on their being maintained. These should be consulted upon and agreed and, thereafter, become non-negotiable. But, so far as possible, the *style* in which those standards are achieved can be much more a matter for the individual, since flair and talent have more in common with style than they do with observation of norms.'

Cadbury's views are echoed by American leadership thinker James McGregor Burns who defines leadership as 'leaders inducing followers to act for certain goals that represent the values and motivations, the wants and needs, the aspirations and expectations - of both leaders and followers'.[2]

There is a general agreement that leaders set the direction and establish the values of any organisation. They are key builders of what is now labelled 'corporate culture'. This is most clearly manifested in the armed services.

'The human side of leadership, certainly in the armed forces, must contain a strong element of

what I call ethos.  It is something which is difficult
to talk about but it is the sort of spirit that motivates
armed forces and is very much part of what makes
people put their lives on the line,' says General Sir
Peter Inge.    'It is certainly not a policy, nor a
science, it is a mixture of emotional, intellectual
and moral qualities.   It is about comradeship and
team spirit; it is about integrity and the high quality
of people one is fortunate to work and serve with
and I emphasise the word serve because I believe
that although monetary reward is important, it is
not a driving force.'

215

Again this central concept is highly abstract and the
actual role played by the leader difficult to establish.    The most significant measure of a leader's
impact can be the simple one of time.

### Leadership in practice: Watson's IBM

Few business people create companies in their own image which then thrive after their departure. Most plummet after the final farewell from the great leader, unable or unwilling to carry on as before. Thomas Watson Senior (1874-1956), the man behind IBM, is one of the rare exceptions. Under Watson, IBM became the stuff of corporate and stock market legend, continuing to dominate long after Watson's death.

Watson created a corporate culture which lasted. IBM - 'Big Blue' - became the archetypal modern corporation and its managers the ultimate stereotype - with their regulation sombre suits, white shirts, plain ties, zeal for selling and company song. Beneath this, however, lay a belief in competing vigorously and providing quality service. Later, competitors complained that IBM's sheer size won it orders. This was only partly true. Its size masked a deeper commitment to managing customer accounts, providing service and building relationships. These elements were established by the demanding perfectionist, Watson.

'He emphasised people and service - obsessively,' noted Tom Peters in *Liberation Management*. 'IBM was a service star in an era of malperforming machines.'

IBM's origins lay in the semantically challenged Computing-Tabulating-Recording Company which Watson joined in 1914. Under Watson the company's revenues doubled from $4.2 million to $8.3 million by 1917. Initially making everything from butcher's scales to meat slicers, its activities gradually concentrated on tabulating machines which processed information mechanically on punched cards. Watson boldly renamed the company International Business Machines. This was, at the time, overstating the company's credentials though IBM Japan was established before the Second World War.

IBM's development was helped by the 1937 Wages-Hours Act which required US companies to record hours worked and wages paid. The existing machines couldn't cope and Watson instigated work on a solution. In 1944 the Mark 1 was launched, followed by the Selective Sequence Electronic Calculator in 1947. By then IBM's revenues were $119 million and it was set to make the great leap forward to become the world's largest computer company.

While Thomas Watson Senior created IBM's culture, his son, Thomas Watson Junior (1914-1994) moved it from being an outstanding performer to world dominance. Watson Jr brought a vision of the future to the company which his father had lacked. Yet, the strength of the original culture remained intact. Indeed, Watson Jr fleshed it out, creating a framework of theories round the intuitive and hard-nosed business acumen of his father.

Typically, Watson Sr made sure his son served a brief apprenticeship - as an IBM salesman - and Watson Jr remained driven by his father's lessons throughout his career. 'The secret I learned early on from my father was to run scared and never think I had made it,' he said. And, sure enough, when IBM thought it had made it the ground slipped beneath its previously sure feet.

In his book, *A Business and Its Beliefs* - an extended IBM mission statement - Watson Jr tellingly observes: "The beliefs that mould great organisations frequently grow out of the character, the experience and the convictions of a single person.' In IBM's case that person was Thomas Watson Senior.

## *The new agenda for leaders*

### 1. Open leadership

'Dynamic leadership...has at its heart both the strength to care and the will to command,' observes Richard Wells in a telling summary of the new agenda facing leaders in the late 1990s and beyond.

Today's leaders embrace a new openness. While arguing that traditional values such as discipline are vital, creating a climate of openness is identified by Sir Raymond Lygo as a core function of leadership. 'Nothing succeeds like success. People need to be touched; lead by example, but admit your faults openly. Give praise in equal measure, at least to admonition. Discipline is a key word that should not be misunderstood; efficient ships are not dirty ships - standards, standards, standards. Be open, give as much information as you can and make sure that promotion in your organisation is based on merit, and seen to be.'

Leadership through dictatorship is regarded as inappropriate and, if attempted, likely to be short-lived. 'Coercion provides leadership of a kind, but it only lasts as long as the force backing it is effective,' says Sir Adrian Cadbury. 'We escape from coercive leadership as soon as we may, because we recognise that we are being used for the leader's benefit. We remain voluntarily under leaders with whose values we identify. We need leaders to set standards which we admire and to which we willingly adhere.'

Even in the armed services General Sir Peter Inge detects a sea-change from command and control to inform and question. 'Leaders nowadays in all walks of life explain the thinking behind decisions and the various options a great deal more than we once did. I don't believe this in any way undermines the fundamentals of leadership and discipline, and indeed it should enhance them. The fundamentals remain in place, but they have been adapted to fit into the practices and expectations of rather different and somewhat demanding times.'

Such basic changes are occurring for a reason. Simply, the old methods of leadership are no longer as effective. The world of the 1990s - whether in business, government or elsewhere - is beset by change and uncertainty. 'The biggest demand on leadership, of course, comes from the management of change. This is one feature which is unquestionably common to every contemporary organisation,' says Valerie Strachan.

Sir John Harvey-Jones, the former ICI chief executive, credited with the company's turnaround in the late 1980s, anticipated this shift: 'Management is not about the preservation of the status quo; it is about maintaining the highest rate of change that the organisation and the people within it can stand.'.

Sir John's words are echoed by a manager at the US company Chaparral Steel who told the *Sloan Management Review:* 'In other companies the word is - don't rock the boat. Here we rock the hell out of the boat. We don't know the factory's limits. We want it to change, to evolve.'[3]

Change is now endemic. 'Leadership used to be about certainty,' observe leadership thinkers Phil Hodgson and Randall White. 'Throughout history (and in the movies), great leaders always appeared to know what to do. The leadership task was about how to get people to where they had to be. Now, however, the most strategically important aspects of an organisation's future lie in the area of **uncertainty**. So the first component that a leader has to learn to do differently is to learn to move **towards** uncertainty rather than away from it.'

To do so, Hodgson and White advocate that leaders 'learn to rely less on copying what others have done in the past. Much of the research and writing on leadership that has been used to guide leaders has been based on past behaviour and not on present and future requirements. Such benchmarking activity is useful, but the best bench-marking can do is bring one up to date'.

In short, the modern leader needs to loosen his or her grip on the need to control. Harvard Business School's Shoshana Zuboff has said that 'learning has replaced control as the fundamental job of management'. And, learning is a far more difficult task to lead or manage effectively.

## 2. Empowering others

The new environment for leaders is characterised by openness and what is now labelled, empowerment. 'Leadership is the ability to get men to do what they don't like to do and like it,' said Harry Truman. Leaders give people the information, the tools and the opportunities to take decisions for themselves. While the theory is neat, the practice is wrought with complications. Empowerment revolutionises the traditional role of the leader. Indeed, in some extreme cases, it has made the leader virtually redundant.

'The leader's responsibility in the organisation is to set people free to create and enable them to generate ideas for their own pursuit of excellence. The bonds which can inhibit innovation come in different shapes,' says Richard Wells in a potent summary of what empowerment involves.

Clinton Silver emphasises that empowerment is not an easy option: 'Treating people fairly and decently does not imply that the company is soft or sloppy. Good human relations are good business. This is a fact which is increasingly acknowledged by business. Companies now seek to involve their employees directly in the running of the business; and acknowledge their broader responsibilities for the environment and society.'

Empowerment brings new definitions of leadership. 'Being a leader is something you do rather than something you are. It is the ability to bring out a number of talents and to operate effectively through other people,' says John Van Marrik in *Discovering the Leader in You.*[4]

Take what has happened at a once obscure Brazilian company, Semco. Semco transports workplace democracy to previously unimagined frontiers. Everyone at the company has access to the books; managers set their own salaries; shopfloor workers set their own productivity targets and schedules; workers make decisions once the preserve of managers; even the distribution of the profit sharing scheme is determined by employees.

'We've taken a company that was moribund and made it thrive, chiefly by refusing to squander our greatest resource, our people,' says chief executive Ricardo Semler. Semler does not regard the transformation of Semco as a lesson to be emulated by other companies. Instead, he believes it simply points to the need for companies and organisations to re-invent themselves for the 1990s. 'There **are** some companies which are prepared to change the way they work. They realise that nothing can be based on what used to be, that there is a better way. But, 99 per cent of companies are not ready, caught in an industrial Jurassic Park.'

As part of Semco's revolution, Semler has to a large extent become redundant. The chief executive's job rotates between five people. Diminished power is clearly not something which fills him with sadness - instead, it is confirmation that the Semco approach works. 'I haven't hired or fired anyone for eight years or signed a company cheque. From an operational side I am no longer necessary, though I still draw a salary because there are many other ways of contributing to the company's success,' he says. Indeed, Semler believes that what many consider the core activity of management - decision making - should not be their function at all. 'It's only when bosses give up decision-making and let their employees govern themselves that the possibility exists for a business jointly managed by workers and executives. That is true participative management.'

Empowerment must be based around trust. 'Trust is critical to leadership. With trust, people grow. Without it, they may perform adequately but higher potential will wither,' says Richard Wells. 'Many front-line staff - not least in the police service - feel that they are **not** trusted. If they feel mistrusted, they feel undervalued. Undervalued people under-produce and under-communicate. Leaders are then isolated from the talent and the feelings of those for whom they work, so creating a spiral of disaffection.'

## From delegation to empowerment

Bold experiments such as Semco's bring into question one of the core skills of leadership: delegation. Traditionally, delegation has always been recognised as a key ingredient of successful management and leadership. In the 1980s, delegation underwent a crisis of confidence - managers were intent on progressing as quickly as possible up the corporate ladder, working 12 hours a day to succeed rather than delegating so that others could share the glory.  In the corporate cut and thrust, delegation appeared to be a sign of weakness.

The 1990s have seen a shift in attitudes.  No longer is delegation an occasional managerial indulgence.  Instead, it has become a necessity.  'With organisations becoming flatter and hierarchies disappearing managers now have a far wider span of control than ever before,' says John Payne, consultant and author of *Letting Go Without Losing Control*.  'In that situation, delegation is vital. The trouble is that delegation is like driving a car - no one admits to being a bad delegator.'

It is not only the fact that many leaders consider themselves to be competent delegators that causes problems. Good delegation is hard work and requires substantial amounts of confidence and faith - leaders, after all, are usually delegating tasks which they are accomplished at carrying out to less experienced people.  'Delegation is being prepared to trust people to do a task and achieve results without your interference,' says John Payne.  'It is easier said than done.  Leaders who make delegation work for them are those who have eliminated fear.  They do not delegate and then sit worrying that the job won't be done well enough and they will be blamed or have to sort it out.  They have confidence in their own position and are not fearful that the person will do too good a job and undermine their position and authority.  Also, they make time to delegate properly.  Initially, delegation does involve committing time, but there are substantial time savings in the near future.'

The trouble is that old habits die hard. Organisations may have shrunk, but managers often remain wedded to habits of a lifetime. 'Many companies are in a state of transition. They have taken layers out of management but haven't yet changed the processes. The remaining managers still have a lot of pressure on them and are often working very long hours,' says Ginny Spittle, a senior human resources manager at ICL. 'The role of managers is changing from controlling and planning to coaching, leading and acting as a resource. If they are to achieve this change they need training and support so they learn to delegate and give full responsibility to people who report to them.'

The need for training and support is one also identified by Richard Phillips of Ashridge Management College. 'People have to come to terms with the fact that they can no longer manage people in a hands-on way any more and dumping trivial tasks on to people is not the best way to delegate,' he says. 'People tend to delegate tasks which they are too busy to do themselves or which they don't want to do themselves. They also tend to delegate them to staff who are judged to be already competent to carry them out to minimise the risk of mistakes and reduce the manager's anxiety levels.'

In short, delegation is a last resort, a worry to the manager doing the delegating and an unwanted extra burden to the person handed the task. But, argues Richard Phillips, it need not be like that. He has carried out extensive research on managers who act as coaches. By doing so, Phillips says, leaders turn conventional wisdom about delegation on its head. 'Instead of selecting someone who can already do the work being delegated, coaches deliberately select someone who cannot do it. In addition to setting the goals of the actual work to be done, they add learning goals. They coach the learner to give them the necessary skills and confidence to carry out the task.'

The need to combine learning, task-fulfilment and delegation is also seen as essential by ICL's Ginny Spittle: 'Managers have to look at more creative approaches. The onus is now on getting the most out of groups and teams of people, but there simply isn't the time to sit down with everyone who reports directly to you. Managers have to delegate successfully so that everyone learns and contributes as the job is done.'

227

Ashridge's Richard Phillips cites an example from a major electronics company he talked to as part of his research on coaching. 'The job of negotiating a large and important maintenance contract was delegated to a senior programmer. There were clear goals, learning objectives and the expectations of both sides were thoroughly aired and discussed beforehand. The end-result was that the manager new to the job learned more about his own company; gained an external perspective; and developed interpersonal and negotiating skills. Not only that - he met the target of reducing the cost of the contract by 10 per cent.'

Of course, the once simple act of delegation has also been hijacked by writers and theorists. Though empowerment is now part of the language of management, genuine examples of it in practice are not always what they may seem. 'With the flattening of hierarchies, empowerment has become a fashionable term. In practice, it is often a synonym for delegation,' warns Dr Ian Cunningham, author of *The Wisdom of Strategic Learning*. Instead of granting genuine power to their staff, managers remain as likely as ever to make the important decisions and only pass on relatively unimportant tasks to others. It is worth remembering that empowerment and delegation are not one and the same. Delegation starts off as part of a manager's job which he or she then delegates. Empowerment, however, involves removing constraints which prevent someone doing their job as effectively as possible.

Empowerment does not automatically make for an easier life. 'It is more difficult to make change happen in an 'empowered' organisation; in many ways it demands more of the leader of the organisation to ensure that people are convinced of the right course, rather than just instructed; but I believe that, once people *are* convinced, the changes will be achieved far more effectively,' says Valerie Strachan.

The danger is that while empowerment attracts the management theorists and fad-following companies delegation remains neglected, its full potential unrealised. A

228

persuasive argument to sit up and take notice comes from Ashridge's Richard Phillips: 'Managers should remember that when they perform a task which someone else could do, they prevent themselves from doing a task which only they could do.'

---

**What does the empowering leader do?**

- emphasises learning rather than authority and control

- enhances and constantly develops the self-esteem of employees

- questions and listens

- builds relationships throughout the organisation

- recognises and acknowledges the role of others

- constantly develops others

- admits errors

- encourages innovation and individual initiative

- develops a flexible vision of the future

- communicates constantly

- coaches and counsels

- trusts

- abides by high ethical standards.

---

### 3. Developing and learning

In the new age, the shackles of organisational structures are being loosened and, sometimes, eliminated. 'Responsibility is not a one-way process,' says Harvard Business School's Chris Argyris. 'We are personally responsible for our behaviour but, unfortunately, many companies change their parking space and not people's sense of responsibility.'

230    Learning and teaching are key factors in creating a more responsible workforce - and the leader is not exempted from this process. Indeed, they must resolve to continually drive it forward. The end result is what is labelled the learning organisation, a concept whose origins can be traced back to Chris Argyris. 'Any company that aspires to succeed in the tougher business environment of the 1990s must first resolve a basic dilemma: success in the marketplace increasingly depends on learning, yet most people don't know how to learn. What's more, those members of the organisation who many assume to be the best at learning are, in fact, not very good at it,' he wrote in a *Harvard Business Review* article. 'Because many professionals are almost always successful at what they do, they rarely experience failure. And because they have rarely failed, they have never learned how to learn from failure'[5]

Argyris' pleasure in the growing interest in the role of learning is combined with fears that it might be short-lived. 'I am pleased that organisational learning is in vogue but I worry that if we are not careful it will become another fad,' he says. 'I have little difficulty in talking about organisational learning to chief executives but, as you go down the hierarchy, it is regarded as being a bit dreamy.'

Argyris' work has exposed some of the defensive routines endemic in leadership practice. In *Knowledge for Action* (1993), Argyris examines the behaviour of one of his consultancy clients, itself a consultancy group. The consultancy arose when seven successful consultants decided to establish their own company. They hoped that it would be free from the Machiavellian political wrangles they had encountered in other organisations. In practice, their dreams were disappointed. Indeed, by the time Argyris was called in, internal wrangling consumed too many of its productive energies.

The anonymous consultants featured in *Knowledge for Action* were, in fact, falling prey to what Argyris calls 'defensive routines'. Faced with a personally threatening problem, the executives were adept at covering it up or by-passing it entirely. Board meetings, therefore, concentrated on trivial topics - there was always one person keen to avoid discussion of an important issue. Outside the boardroom the big issues were discussed and blame apportioned so that divisions built up relentlessly between the original founders. This approach affected the behaviour of the rest of the organisation - others consciously kept information to a minimum so that executives weren't forced to face up to something new.

The fact that Argyris' client is a group of management consultants helps convey the importance of his message. If highly trained, intelligent executives fall into such traps, what chance have ordinary mortals?

The first challenge for many is simply to learn to learn. The leaders noticeably:

- **learn from past experience** - they regard the past as a rich source of achievements to be emulated; mistakes to be learned from; and from people who's own attitudes and approach can be learned from.

- **acknowledge mobility** - the leaders believe that management and learning are never stationary. Today's accomplishments are tomorrow's failings.

- **integrate skills** - learning is not simply a matter of accumulating skill after skill. Instead, it is a question of how they work together and how you utilise them.

- **acknowledge learning as a key part of any job**

- **create an environment in which learning is encouraged and cultivated**

- **learn from everyone and everything.**

In practice the message from the leaders is that learning involves:

- **acknowledging and learning from mistakes**

  As Chris Argyris' work shows, managers fed on a diet of corporate politics are highly adept at covering their footsteps. More often than not, mistakes are covered up and concealed rather than learned from.

'Leadership and management are in many respects the application of common sense, though this needs to be combined with humility and a willingness to recognise your own fallibility and that of others. Good leaders acknowledge their mistakes,' says Sir Colin Marshall.

It is something supported by General Sir Peter Inge: 'Central also to leadership must be a willingness to allow people to make mistakes to encourage their development and to learn from those mistakes. This requires flexibility. Although the great leaders, such as Slim and Montgomery, were notable for their willpower, they also never allowed it to become blind stubbornness.'

American psychologist David McClelland divides people into two broad categories. The first are those motivated by a need for positive achievement. They tend to look on their errors as an opportunity to do better next time. The others, motivated by fear of failure, are typically preoccupied by the need to avoid making mistakes.

In fact the only thing leaders have to fear is fear itself. Psychologist Michael Frese of Giessen University in Germany has carried out research into mistake making. He concludes that pressure leads to mistakes; more pressure, more mistakes. In training, he suggests, people should be set tasks so complicated that they are bound to make mistakes. The result, says Frese, is that people learn more complex skills faster and, though errors are made, their effects are less damaging.

Robert Haas of Levi Strauss has poignantly summed up the new outlook. Describing his approach at Levi Strauss, he says: 'Senior managers try to be explicit about the bad decisions we've made. It de-mystifies senior management and resolves the stigma traditionally associated with taking risks. We also talk about the limitations of our own knowledge, mostly by inviting other people's perspectives.'[6]

♦ **sharing knowledge**

Sir David Gillmore, himself a former teacher, observes: 'A leader has to teach to some extent. Indeed, the current preoccupation in the business world is with the learning organisation - in which senior managers are coaches, mentors and teachers as opposed to narrowly-defined bosses. Leadership is, therefore, not dictatorship but about sharing knowledge and expertise and enabling those who follow to achieve their full potential.'

It is something which is exemplified by Marks and Spencer's approach. 'At M&S there is a culture of communication,' says Clinton Silver. 'This does not mean working by committee, but talking (and listening) to each other. We want people to learn so that they can understand and communicate to others inside and outside the company.'

◆ **asking questions**

Marketing guru Ted Levitt says. 'You have to expose yourself to your environment and ask questions to develop your sensitivity and sensibility. I see things all the time. I go into factories, offices, stores and look out the window and just see things and ask Why? Why are they doing that? Why are things this way and not that? You ask questions and pretty soon you come up with answers. When you begin to try to answer your own questions you become much more receptive to reading things which help you to answer questions. Seeing is one thing but perception requires cognitive effort and personal involvement. You bring something to what you see.'

235

Aware of their limitations, the leaders continually question themselves, their colleagues, subordinates and superiors. Asking questions - and listening to answers - is a very basic skill. Says Sir Adrian Cadbury: 'Leaders need to listen - an underrated art - and to understand the aims and motivation of those they are leading. True leadership is not about issuing commands from on high, but giving precision and form to the aspirations of those being led.'

The most acute observation is that of Chris Argyris that 'to question someone else's reasoning is not a sign of mistrust but a valuable opportunity for learning'.

◆ **developing others**

The preoccupation with succession planning is just one example of how the leaders place emphasis on developing others in their organisation.

Research in 50 of the world's leading companies by Philip Sadler and Keith Milmer highlighted ten important rules for the management of talent:

1. Provide a clear sense of direction and purpose for employees, developing and implementing a strong sense of mission.

2. Develop an appropriately flexible organisational framework, balancing control and creativity, and integrating different procedural and value systems.

3. Understand the company culture and nurture the talented people within it through the authority of expertise, encouraging innovation and risk-taking, providing freedom, autonomy, space and flexibility, openness and trust, and a dedication to excellence.

4. Clearly identify future requirements for talent, both quantitatively and qualitively.

5. Create a talent pool by developing recruitment and selection strategies.

6. Identify high potential.

7. Build ties of loyalty and commitment; these are often more important than financial incentives.

8. Set clear objectives and ensure that they are met, providing support at all levels.

9. Motivate and develop talented people.

10. Continuously evaluate the impact of human resource strategies in terms of cost-benefit analysis and employee attitudes and satisfaction.

237

Perhaps the best summary of the skills required from leaders in the future comes from Sir Peter Parker. He says leaders will:

- take risks and be professional.

- educate and build teams

- be international in experience, practice and outlook.

- be political animals.

- be citizens.

**Leadership in practice:**
*The Royal Mail Leadership Charter*

Few organisations take leadership seriously enough to actually articulate its role in the organisation and their views on what makes for good leadership. One of the exceptions is the Royal Mail. It has developed a Leadership Charter which identifies the behaviour it believes is vital for its mission and values to be achieved. These are:

*Vision*

A leader:

- provides a clear vision which aligns with the mission and values and captures the imagination
- describes the vision in simple language and frequently checks understanding
- translates the vision into measurable goals that stretch the leader and the team and also challenge convention.

*Commitment*

A leader:

- takes on ownership of ideas adopted by the business whatever the prior debate
- demonstrates consistent and constant personal commitment to the vision through appropriate

allocation of resources and the use of personal time
- ◆ secures the personal commitment of immediate colleagues
- ◆ places emphasis on gaining enthusiastic acceptance as well as directing the process of change.

*Management Approach*

Leaders create a success culture by emphasising behaviours under the following headings:

### 1. People

A leader places emphasis on:

- ◆ recognition
- ◆ participation and involvement
- ◆ respect, caring, trust and openness
- ◆ safety and security
- ◆ setting clear accountabilities
- ◆ creation of a controlled risk-taking culture
- ◆ empowerment
- ◆ preparedness to take decisions
- ◆ training and development
- ◆ feedback, coaching and counselling
- ◆ team working
- ◆ promoting the highest standards of behaviour
- ◆ creating and innovation.

## 2. Business Performance

A leader places emphasis on:

- providing added value to the customer
- setting high minimum standards
- continuous performance improvements
- measurement of outputs and performance
- creating functional working
- flexibility in meeting changing customer requirements
- decision making based on facts and analysis
- reviewing progress against agreed objectives

## 3. Personal Contribution

A leader places emphasis on:

- upholding Royal Mail values
- demonstrating a strong outward focus through benchmarking and personal contact with customers and hence the community
- displaying high personal levels of competence and judgement, caring and integrity
- being accessible and visible
- accepting personal accountability

*Communication*

A leader:

- identifies the communication implications of every policy, decision and situation
- plans the communication activity including the definition, consistency, regularity and timing of the key messages
- uses a range of channels while placing a particular emphasis on face to face: is open, honest and positive
- seeks input and listens carefully
- uses measurements to ensure the consistency and effectiveness of the communication process.

*References*

1. Bennis, W, 'Managing the dream', *Training Magazine*, 1990

2. Burns, James MacGregor, *Leadership*, Harper & Row, New York, 1978

3. 'The factory as a learning laboratory', *Sloan Management Review*, May-June 1991

4. Marrik, John Van, *Discovering the Leader in You*, McGraw Hill, Maidenhead, 1994

5.    Argyris, C, 'Teaching smart people how to learn', *Harvard Business Review*, May-June 1991

6.    'Values make the company', *Harvard Business Review*, September-October 1990

# Understanding

# Leadership

---

Leadership thinking has lurched from one theory to another. The main schools of thought can be divided into:

- ◆ **Great Man Theory**

  Great Man theories were the stuff of the late nineteenth and early twentieth centuries, though their residue remains in much popular thinking on the subject. The Great Man theory is based round the idea that the leader is born with innate, unexplainable and, for mere mortals, incomprehensible leadership skills. They are, therefore, elevated as heroes.

  This theory is now of limited validity, not least because Great Men must now include Great Women. It is based round the basic idea that the leader is right and leadership is based on the authority of their righteousness. It thrives on the subjugation of followers rather than their empowerment.

◆ **Trait Theory**

This theory continues to fill numerous volumes. If you know who the Great Men are, you can then examine their personalities and behaviour to develop traits of leaders. This is plausible, but deeply flawed. For all the books attempting to identify common traits among leaders there is little correlation. While one hefty study may conclude that communication is vital, another is likely to select vision as the vital ingredient in becoming a successful leader. A steady flow of such books continue to emerge.

◆ **Power and Influence Theory**

This approach chooses to concentrate on the networks of power and influence generated by the leader. It is, however, based on the assumption that all roads lead to the leader and negates the role of followers and the strength of organisational culture.

◆ **Behaviourist Theory**

In some ways the behaviourist school continues to hold sway. It emphasises what leaders actually do rather than their characteristics. Its advocates include Blake and Mouton (creators of the Managerial Grid) and Rensis Likert. The end-result of a great deal of research tends to come up with idyllic lists of leadership styles.

- ◆ **Situational Theory**

  Situational Theory views leadership as specific to a situation rather than a particular sort of personality. It is based round the plausible notion that different circumstances require different forms of leadership. Its champions include Kenneth Blanchard and Paul Hersey whose influential book, *Situational Leadership Theory* remains a situationalist manifesto.

- ◆ **Contingency Theory**

  Developing from Situational Theory, contingency approaches attempt to elect situational variables which best indicate the most appropriate leadership style to suit the circumstances. Fred Fiedler, for example, found the critical factors of a leadership situation to be leader-member relations, task structure and the position power of the leader.

- ◆ **Transactional Theory**

  Increasingly fashionable, Transactional Theory places emphasis on the relationship between leaders and followers. It examines the mutual benefit from an exchange-based relationship with the leader offering certain things, such as resources or rewards, in return for others, such as the followers' commitment or acceptance of the leader's authority.

- ◆ **Attribution Theory**

  This elevates followership to new importance, concentrating on the factors which lie behind the followers' attribution of leadership to a particular leader.

- ◆ **Transformational Theory**

  While transactional leadership models are based on the extrinsic motivation of an exchange relationship, transformational leadership is based on intrinsic motivation. As such, the emphasis is on commitment rather than compliance from the followers. The transformational leader is, therefore, a pro-active, innovative, visionary. With the continuing preoccupation with managing change, this is the most potent of the current crop of theories.

# FURTHER READING

Adair, John, *Effective Leadership: A Modern Guide to Developing Leadership Skills,* Pan, London, 1988

Bass, Bernard, & Avolio, Bruce, *Improving Organizational Effectiveness Through Transformational leadership,* Sage, London, 1994

Bennis, Warren, *Leaders: The Strategies for Taking Charge* (with Burt Nanus), Harper & Row, New York, 1985

Bennis, Warren, *On Becoming a Leader*, Addison-Wesley, Reading, 1989

Bennis, Warren, *Why leaders can't lead*, Jossey-Bass, San Francisco, 1989

Bennis, Warren, *An Invented Life: Reflections on Leadership and Change*, Addison-Wesley, Reading, 1993

Blake, Robert, & Mouton, Jane, *The Managerial Grid: Key Orientations for Achieving Production Through People,* Gulf, Houston, 1964

Burns, James MacGregor, *Leadership,* Harper & Row, New York, 1978

Christopher, Elizabeth, and Smith, Larry, *Leadership Training: A Sourcebook of Activities,* Kogan Page, London, 1993

Fiedler, Fred, and Chemers, Martin, *Improving Leadership Effectiveness: The Leader Match Concept,* John Wiley, New York, 1984

Fiedler, Fred, & Chemers, Martin, *Leadership and Effective Management,* Scott Firesman, Glenview, Illinois, 1974

248    Graham, Pauline (editor), *Mary Parker Follett Prophet of Management,* Harvard Business School Press, Boston, 1994

Kotter, John, *A Force for Change: How Leadership Differs From Management,* Free Press, New York, 1990

Leavy, Brian, & Wilson, David, *Strategy and Leadership,* John Wiley, London, 1994

Maucher, Helmut, *Leadership in Action: Tough Minded Strategies from the Global Giant,* McGraw Hill, New York, 1994

Morris, Steve and Willcocks, Graham, *How to Lead a Winning Team,* IM/Pitman Publishing, London, 1995

O'Connor, Carol, *Successful Leadership in a Week,* Headway, London, 1994

Reddin, William, *The Best of Bill Reddin,* IPM, London, 1985

Syrett, Michel, and Hogg, Clare (editors), *Frontiers of Leadership: An Essential Reader,* Blackwell, Oxford, 1992

White, RP, Hodgon, P and Crainer, S, *White Water Leadership*, FT/Pitman, London, 1996

Wright, Peter, and Taylor, David, *Improving Leadership Performance: Interpersonal Skills for Effective Leadership,* Prentice Hall, London, 1994

Yukl, Gary, *Leadership in Organizations,* (2nd edition), Prentice Hall, Englewood Cliffs, New Jersey, 1989

Zaleznik, Abraham, *The Managerial Mystique: Restoring Leadership in Business,* Harper & Row, New York, 1990

# INDEX

## A

## B